Spices & Lime

Spices & Lime

Recipes from a Modern South East Asian Kitchen

Shamsydar Ani

Marshall Cavendish
Cuisine

To my beloved Sambal Prince, Irfan Helmi.

Text and photographs by Shamsydar Ani
Editor: Lo Yi Min
Designer: Bernard Go

Copyright © 2021 Marshall Cavendish International (Asia) Pte Ltd

Published by Marshall Cavendish Cuisine
An imprint of Marshall Cavendish International

A member of the
Times Publishing Group

Other Marshall Cavendish Offices:
Marshall Cavendish Corporation, 800 Westchester Ave, Suite N-641, Rye Brook, NY 10573, USA •
Marshall Cavendish International (Thailand) Co Ltd, 253 Asoke, 16th Floor, Sukhumvit 21 Road,
Klongtoey Nua, Wattana, Bangkok 10110, Thailand • Marshall Cavendish (Malaysia) Sdn Bhd,
Times Subang, Lot 46, Subang Hi-Tech Industrial Park, Batu Tiga, 40000 Shah Alam,
Selangor Darul Ehsan, Malaysia

Marshall Cavendish is a registered trademark of Times Publishing Limited

National Library Board, Singapore Cataloguing in Publication Data

Name(s): Shamsydar Ani.
Title: Spices & lime : recipes from a modern South East Asian kitchen /
    Shamsydar Ani.
Description: Singapore : Marshall Cavendish Cuisine, [2020]
Identifier(s): OCN 1184238387 | ISBN 978-981-48-6851-8 (paperback)
Subject(s): LCSH: Cooking, Malay. | Halal food. | LCGFT: Cookbooks.
Classification: DDC 641.59595--dc23

Printed in Singapore

contents

introduction

I have always proudly been a Singaporean Malay – I cannot run away from being identified as Malay and Muslim, especially since I have a tan and I pretty much wear my religion on my head. Oftentimes, though, I get comments from people I meet, saying that I either speak with an accent or that I have adventurous taste buds. I blame too much American TV for the former and my family for the latter.

Raising five children during the '90s in Singapore was not the easiest thing for my parents to do. Though I am the youngest of my siblings and can't recall my early years as vividly, I remember that we did not eat out a lot. We always had dinner at home, while restaurant meals were reserved for special occasions. I don't think I missed out much though. Apart from occasional midnight suppers of prata, *sup tulang* (a delicious red stew made with beef bone) and durians, I vaguely remember eating things my friends never heard of.

Being Malay also means being fed your standard array of nasi Padang dishes as a child, day in, day out. Rice is a staple, and God forbid the rice container in the pantry should ever be empty, or all hell would break loose. Splashes of oil and *rempah* (spice paste) around the stove were common, and proteins such as chicken and fish were always fried. My mother's old Baby Belling oven would sit nicely on the kitchen countertop, only to be used during Hari Raya Aidilfitri (Eid) when she would make *kek lapis* (layer cake), *kek buah* (fruit cake) and *kek marble* (marble cake).

Being raised by a Malay mother means that you're expected to help around the house but never in the kitchen. The kitchen was always her territory – enter it when she is cooking and you'll end up getting scolded without even knowing why. Try even breathing in her direction, towards the kitchen, and you'll incur her wrath. I really do love my mother, but not when she's in the kitchen. I vaguely remember being tasked to peel eggs as she prepared the sambal on the stove one time, but I ended up eating the eggs because I was too hungry. I avoided being in the kitchen with my mum after that, until I was in my late teens at least.

But of course, having four daughters meant that my mother had to share her kitchen sooner or later, even if she wasn't the one teaching us to cook. My eldest sister, Shamsynar, became the first in our family to study abroad. Having to live on her own, my dearest sister had to learn to cook because living on government scholarship wasn't much and Malay food was hard to come by in the UK. When she came home, she brought along with her a copy of Jamie Oliver's *The Naked Chef*. One of the foods she first served us was a simple dish – pasta *aglio olio* (pasta with garlic and oil). She went on to make bolognese and, eventually, lasagna, which became her signature dish. This was way before there were any halal Italian restaurants around in Singapore!

In 2009, we made a trip to Vietnam as a family, and Shamsynar, who organised the trip, made sure there were some good local restaurants we could try. As usual, she came back eager to make pho like the ones we had in Vietnam. Needless to say, I never eat lasagna and beef pho unless they are made by my sister.

Then there's my second sister, Malisa, the disciplinarian and baker. She picked up baking and began making cakes, brownies and cookies. She had a few cookbooks that she kept high up on the bookshelf, but I was tall enough to stand on my toes and reach for them, just so that I could gawk and drool at photographs of cakes. Malisa developed a specialty in making American-style cheesecakes, and she dragged me into the kitchen to help with preparing them. I was always tasked with crushing digestive biscuits and cracking eggs, since these required minimal effort and I couldn't possibly eat raw eggs. I had not written down the recipes nor seen her write them down herself, but thanks to my elephant's memory, at least one of them is forever recorded for years to come in this book. Though I complained about the times I unwillingly spent in the kitchen with her, I did manage to get my hands on some of her signature recipes, which have indeed been helpful since her move to the United States years ago.

My third sister, Mira, was the only one allowed to take Food and Nutrition, also known as Home Economics, as an examinable subject in school. She would come home from school with containers of food and bakes she made in school and have me devour them. With her lessons as her springboard, she would make cheap cheats of otherwise expensive and tedious recipes. Being entrepreneurial, Mira later began selling her bakes and dishes while working as a stay-at-home-mum.

Finally, the matriarch – my mother, my Ibu. My mother routinely cooks a repertoire of Malay dishes: *ayam masak merah* (spicy tomato chicken), *ayam lemak cili padi* (chicken in coconut cream with bird's eye chilli), beef rendang, *kuah celok* (assam vegetable soup), *kari ayam* (chicken curry) and so on. Occasionally, Ibu would surprise us all with a dish she consider the most tedious, her *laksa ikan tenggiri* (laksa with Spanish mackerel), complete with *sambal telur burung* (quail eggs in sweet and spicy sambal). Some weekends, we woke up to *nasi lemak* (rice cooked in coconut cream and served with sides) ready for breakfast. These Malay dishes made my childhood, and they are the ones I keep coming back to because of familiarity, comfort and nostalgia. I remember the excitement I would feel when arriving home from school. Taking in the aroma of spices wafting through the air, I would scream at the door while taking my shoes off, "DID YOU COOK MY FAVOURITE LEMAK CILI PADI TODAY?!", and take comfort in knowing that my mother was at home.

It is no surprise that I grew up a chubby child, always the odd one out in school, prioritising recess over the mandatory Trim and Fit (TAF) Club that all overweight students were forced to attend. In secondary school, I joined a competitive sport – canoeing – and went on to win medals and trophies for the school, yet I was still the big girl who would run from the classroom to the canteen to queue for halal fishball noodles. I got into trouble once when I skipped TAF Club and persuaded a few other members to join me in having those fishball noodles. Needless to say, my teachers are probably having a laugh right now because they already knew that nothing could come between my food and me.

My love for food would not exist if not for the family that raised me. As much as my family is a difficult one to live with, it is through food that we make amends after fights, arguments and silly misunderstandings. Birthdays are always celebrated with cake, candles and a dinner of our favourite dishes. The fasting month of Ramadhan and Eidulfitri always bring with them copious amounts of food, and the table becomes the centre of attraction. Public holidays like Christmas, which we don't even celebrate, become days for us to gather and have more food. We may not receive expensive gifts, but food is always in abundance at home. Food has and will always be our love language.

I'm also thankful for a husband who loves food and actually gives me constructive comments and suggestions on how to make my food better. I'm glad I married into a family of good cooks, with my mother-in-law and her sisters being wonderful cooks, especially when it comes to traditional North Indian cuisine.

Now that I'm married and with my own little family, I hope to continue the food traditions I hadn't realised that my family had been practising. These recipes passed down from my mother and sisters to me, tricks we learnt from watching Jamie Oliver or reading cooking blogs, and cooking techniques we learnt from each other shall be taught to my little ones. In the meantime, this book will serve as an encyclopaedia of sorts for my family's favourite recipes from around the world.

I hope the recipes in this book create new memories for you and your loved ones, just as how writing this book has led me through a journey of rediscovering my roots and understanding where this insatiable appetite for non-local food comes from. This book is merely a guide; substitute ingredients as you feel suitable, add your own twist, and most importantly, cook from the heart no matter how corny it sounds.

Shamsydar Ani

understanding how the halal diet works

Similar to the kosher diet, the halal diet requires meat to be slaughtered Islamically by reciting "Bismillahirrahmanirrahim" (In the name of God, the most compassionate and merciful) before the animal's life is taken in a humane manner by slitting its jugular vein. By saying the Basmallah, the animal calms down as it takes its last breath and faces its fate which has been pre-determined by God. Slitting the animal at the jugular vein ensures a painless, instant death without any forms of torture.

Apart from swine, Muslims are prohibited from eating meats of amphibians and pests, as well as consuming alcohol. Any food items, ingredients or chemicals derived from non-halal sources are also prohibited. Now, you're probably wondering how, then, do Muslims eat out or enjoy food? The answer is pretty simple — we choose to eat natural foods and prefer snacks that have ingredient lists we as laypeople understand. It's a lot easier to eat out when you're in Muslim majority countries like Malaysia or Indonesia and in the Middle East. In Singapore, a lot of food establishments are halal-certified; this allows Muslims to consume their food without any doubts or worry.

When I travel to Europe, the Americas and Australia, though, I tend to go pescatarian or vegetarian. Since there is an increasing demand for vegan food, it's even easier for Muslims to eat out when travelling. Most of the times though, it's more fun to explore the local halal butchery and cook on our own. Produce in different countries often excite me since locally grown produce is always fresher and there is a variety of fruits and vegetables to choose from. Some of my favourite cuisines to draw on when cooking for my family are Italian, French (their desserts!) and hearty Moroccan.

Islam is a relatively easy religion, and while our dietary restrictions make it challenging to join in the fun sometimes, eating as naturally as possible makes it possible to enjoy food. If all else fails, you can always refer to this book if you're craving for some foods that aren't traditionally halal.

what's in a modern kitchen

A kitchen belonging to a woman of my mother's generation is typically a mix of mess and tidiness. More often than not, countertops are filled with a standard array of kitchen appliances – a small toaster, a hot water dispenser, a rice cooker, a Baby Belling oven and a food processor. The cupboards store brown vintage plates, Pyrex serving wares, Corelle plates and Tupperware containers with mismatched lids. The stove and sink are always clean and tidy, but perhaps not so in the pantry, where canned goods of yesteryears and dried goods from aeons ago sit amongst the array of snacks, flours and sugars.

Fresh herbs and aromatics such as *daun limau kasturi* (calamansi lime leaf), *daun kunyit* (turmeric leaf) and *serai* (lemongrass) are purchased at the wet market. It's very likely that only three kinds of onions can be found in the pantry: red onions, shallots and garlic, which we call *bawang putih* (literally translated as white onion). As for potatoes, expect only waxy ones from the neighbourhood provision shop to be stocked, and rice would be either basmati or jasmine rice. The classic Kicap Cap Kipas (Fan brand soy sauce), both the sweet and salty versions, are also likely staples. And of course, chillies in every colour and size are always, always kept refrigerated, while dried chillies live with the other dried goods in the cupboard.

The modern kitchen, however, is a lot more organised, well maintained and definitely diversified. Countertops are kept clear of many appliances, as technology allows us to have smaller, multi-functional ones instead. I have not used a rice cooker for close to a decade now, since the one at my mother's broke down many years ago. I find it a joy to cook rice on the stove – it is one of the most basic cooking techniques one should master. Spices are decanted into jars or clear containers, complete with custom labels so it's easy to see what's available or running out at a glance.

Pantries are now not just stocked with the standard array of Asian dried goods. Japanese short grain rice and Italian Arborio rice join the basmati and jasmine rice on the shelf. Yellow and white onions also share pantry space with the red onions, shallots and garlic. Cooking methods do not just involve long hours on the stove, but instead include chucking things in the oven to save time and effort. Other methods of cooking, like braising and grilling are embraced, making traditional recipes even more delicious and worth the time and effort.

#imalay

My mother is a pure Boyanese since both my maternal grandparents came from the island of Bawean, Indonesia. My father is of Minang descent, and his parents also came from Indonesia, albeit the city of Padang in West Sumatra. One particular dish that the Minang are known for is rendang Minang, a hearty beef stew cooked in spices and coconut milk. Not being biased, but my mother, the Boyanese, makes the best rendang Minang around. Of course, being me, I have to elevate it a bit more by using one of the more expensive beef cuts — beef cheek — instead of the cheaper beef chuck. I've also made the recipe simpler by using the oven instead of letting the dish cook over the stove.

IBU'S BOUJEE RENDANG MINANG

Serves 6

INGREDIENTS

2 Tbsp cumin seeds

2 Tbsp fennel seeds

1 Tbsp coriander seeds

1 star anise

5 cloves

2 sticks cinnamon

3 large red onions, peeled

1 head garlic, peeled

2.5-knob ginger, peeled

50 g bird's eye chillies (*cili padi*)

100 g red chillies

50 g dried red chillies

2 knobs galangal, 2.5-cm each, peeled

5 candlenuts

4 stalks lemongrass

1 kg beef cheek, cut into 2.5-cm chunks

Salt as needed

Vegetable oil as needed

1 turmeric leaf

8 kaffir lime leaves

500 ml fresh coconut milk

50 g tamarind paste, diluted with 50 ml water

METHOD

1. Toast cumin, fennel and coriander seeds with star anise, cloves and cinnamon in a dry frying pan over medium heat until fragrant. Place toasted spices in a food processor together with onions, garlic, ginger, all the chillies, a knob of galangal, candlenuts and 3 stalks lemongrass. Blend until a fine paste forms. You may have to add a dash of water if the paste is too thick but not as fine. Set aside.

2. Drain excess water from the beef and pat dry with paper towels. Place on a tray and sprinkle liberally with salt. This helps the beef absorb flavours as well as makes it tender. Set aside until the *rempah* (spice paste) is cooked.

3. Preheat the oven to 160°C.

4. In a Dutch oven over medium heat, add enough vegetable oil to cover the base of the pot. Once the oil is hot, add blended paste and sauté until it has dried up, or when the oil starts to separate from the paste. This takes 15–20 minutes on medium-low heat. This process of *pecah minyak* (breaking the oil) is crucial in making the rendang. Be patient and continue stirring and sautéing the spices.

5. Add the remaining lemongrass and galangal, as well as the turmeric and lime leaves, then sauté for another 5 minutes. Add beef and stir to coat with the *rempah* before pouring in coconut milk. Stir once more, cover the pot, then place in the oven and cook for 2 hours. After an hour, stir the rendang, scraping the bottom of the pot to ensure nothing sticks. Cover the pot and let it finish cooking.

6. Remove the rendang from the oven, add tamarind juice and season with salt as desired. Serve with white rice.

Fried chicken is my Achilles heel. Whenever I was on a diet or trying to lose weight, I could never say no to fried chicken. I've since found ways to indulge in this favourite comfort food of mine only occasionally, and that's when I make the marinade from scratch. This crispy spiced fried chicken is best paired with a piping hot plate of *nasi lemak* along with *sambal tumis* (see page 19 for both recipes). Ahh, that's the kind of big breakfast I look forward to on weekends.

AYAM GORENG BEREMPAH

Serves 6

INGREDIENTS

1 whole chicken, cut into 12 pieces

1 Tbsp + 1 tsp salt

200 ml fresh coconut milk

1 tsp coriander seeds

1 tsp cumin seeds

1 large red onion, peeled

3 cloves garlic, peeled

2.5-cm knob ginger, peeled

2 stalks lemongrass, chopped

3 Tbsp dried chilli paste

$1/2$ tsp ground turmeric

1 tsp cornflour

Enough vegetable oil for deep frying

METHOD

1. Prepare chicken pieces by cleaning and patting them dry with paper towels. Place in a large bowl and sprinkle liberally with a tablespoonful of salt. Let them rest for about 30 minutes in the refrigerator before soaking the chicken in coconut milk. Marinate for at least an hour in the refrigerator.

2. Toast coriander and cumin seeds in a dry frying pan until fragrant. Place toasted spices in a food processor together with onion, garlic, ginger, lemongrass, chilli paste, ground turmeric and a teaspoonful of salt. Blend until a thick, smooth paste forms. Do not add any water to the blended spices as it will affect the texture of the paste.

3. Add blended paste and cornflour to the marinating chicken and mix thoroughly. Cover and let rest in the refrigerator for 1–2 hours or overnight, if possible, to allow the chicken to absorb all the flavours.

4. Heat a heavy-bottomed pot filled halfway with vegetable oil. Once the oil is hot, turn the heat to low and fry chicken pieces for about 5 minutes on each side. Do this in batches to avoid overcrowding the pot. The low heat ensures that the chicken remains juicy and moist but crispy outside.

5. Serve as a side with a main dish of your choice.

In recent times, some food establishments have sought to elevate the humble *nasi lemak*. Often served for breakfast, this is a kampung dish of coconut rice served with an omelette, *sambal tumis* (sweet sambal) and a medley of crispy fried peanuts and *ikan bilis*. It comes from humble origins — all the ingredients are pantry staples, which means you do not need any fancy meats to cook it. Whenever I crave it, I make it at home instead of buying some. It only takes an hour and this one-dish meal is sure to keep you full for hours.

NASI LEMAK

Serves 4

INGREDIENTS

200 g basmati rice

400 g water (or use the Asian finger method explained in the first step)

3-cm knob ginger, peeled and lightly smashed

1 stalk lemongrass, white part only

100 ml fresh coconut milk

1 tsp salt

SAMBAL TUMIS

2 medium red onions, peeled

10 cloves garlic, peeled

3-cm knob ginger, peeled

1 Tbsp dried anchovies (*ikan bilis*), rinsed and drained

4 Tbsp vegetable oil

2 Tbsp dried chilli paste

1 tsp dried prawn paste (*belacan*)

1 tsp tamarind paste

1 tsp sugar

Salt to taste

TO SERVE

Fried eggs

Sliced cucumbers

Crispy fried anchovies

Ayam goreng berempah (page 18)

METHOD

1. To prepare the rice, rinse at least 3 times under running tap water. You can measure out 400 g water for the rice, but I find that the Asian finger method is best. Stick your index finger into the pot to touch the top of the rice, then add water until it reaches the first joint of your finger. Place ginger and lemongrass in the pot as well.

2. Cook the rice on the stove over medium-low heat, covered, for about 15 minutes. Once most of the water is absorbed, add coconut milk and salt, then stir once. Do not stir the rice excessively as you do not want starch to build up. Cook for another 5-10 minutes over medium heat, until all the liquid is absorbed. Turn off the heat and leave the rice uncovered for at least 10 minutes before serving.

3. To prepare the sambal, place onions, garlic, ginger and dried anchovies in a blender and blend until a smooth paste forms. You may have to add a dash of water to help in the blending.

4. Heat oil in a medium pot. Once the oil is hot, sauté blended paste until it has been tempered, or when the oil starts to separate from the spices. As with all Malay recipes, a well-tempered *rempah* (spice paste) helps flavours develop nicely. Add dried chilli paste and dried prawn paste, then fry over low heat for 3-5 minutes before adding tamarind paste, sugar and salt. If you'd like to add a protein, such as boiled quail eggs, grilled prawns or fish balls, add it in now. Fry for another 3-4 minutes, or until the proteins are cooked.

5. Serve the rice with *sambal tumis*, a fried egg, cucumber slices, crispy fried anchovies and *ayam goreng berempah*.

As a child, I was scared of anything spicy. My mum had to train me to eat spicy food because she wanted to make sure I could eat whatever she cooked for the rest of the family so that she wouldn't have to cook a separate dish for me. I began loving this Minang-style sambal when I was a teenager, and I'd constantly tell my mum that it wasn't spicy enough. Funnily, it got to a point where she once cooked a separate bowl of spicier sambal just for me.

SAMBAL BELADO

Serves 6

INGREDIENTS

2.5-cm knob ginger, peeled

1 head garlic, peeled

5 Tbsp vegetable oil

3 stalks lemongrass

5 kaffir lime leaves

500 g red chillies, coarsely chopped

100 g bird's eye chillies, (*cili padi*) coarsely chopped

2 tomatoes, chopped (optional)

Juice of 1 lime

Salt to taste

METHOD

1. Place ginger and garlic in a food processor and blend until a smooth paste forms. You may have to add a dash of water if the paste is too thick.

2. Heat oil in a medium wok. Do not add too much oil because you do not want an oily sambal. Sauté ginger-garlic paste until fragrant and tempered well. Add lemongrass and lime leaves, then cook for 5-10 minutes on low heat.

3. Add both chillies to the wok and continue frying until everything is well combined. If you prefer a less spicy sambal, add tomatoes and fry for 20 minutes. Add lime juice and season well with salt.

4. Serve as a condiment or add fried chicken to the sambal. This sambal is very versatile; it also goes with proteins such as prawns, fish and grilled beef. It can be stored in a jar and kept in the back of the refrigerator for up to 3 months.

When my friends say they are scared of cooking Malay food, I tell them the dishes are actually very easy. The most difficult part is in the prep work, where you peel the aromatics and blend or chop them, toast the spices, and the list goes on. I grew up watching my mother prep the spices and aromatics once a week, when she spends a day in the kitchen blending the onions, ginger, garlic and whatnots, then storing them in empty jars she's collected. Being a working mother, this helped my mum save lots of time in the kitchen, and she never left for work without preparing food for us. This trick of mine uses the *sambal belado* (Minang-style sambal) I shared and turns it into a hearty main dish for dinner.

PLAY CHEAT AYAM LEMAK CHILLI PADI

Serves 5

INGREDIENTS

1 whole kampung chicken, about 1 kg, cut into 8 pieces

Salt as needed

1 tsp ground turmeric

3 Tbsp *sambal belado* (page 23)

1 turmeric leaf

3 kaffir lime leaves

100 g fresh coconut milk

1 tsp lime juice

METHOD

1. Prepare chicken pieces by cleaning and patting them dry with paper towels. Place in a large bowl and salt liberally, then let them rest for about an hour in the refrigerator.

2. After an hour, preheat the oven to 200°C on the grill setting. Rub $1/2$ teaspoonful of ground turmeric all over the chicken pieces, then arrange on a baking tray and grill for about 20 minutes. Remove from the oven and set aside.

3. In a medium-sized pot over medium heat, add *sambal belado*, turmeric and lime leaves, and the remaining ground turmeric. Sauté for 3-4 minutes until fragrant. Add chicken pieces and coconut milk, then let simmer on a gentle low heat for about 10 minutes.

4. Stir in lime juice and season with a teaspoonful of salt. Turn off the heat and serve with white rice.

Whenever I shoot weddings on weekends, I look forward to my lunch break as I usually get pampered with great food. *Nasi minyak* (ghee rice) is a dish served at Malay weddings, and though it may be simple to cook, few caterers actually get it right. I love *nasi minyak* that's light, fluffy and well seasoned with spices. During the fasting month when there are usually no weddings, I'll cook this and serve it with *ayam masak merah* (spicy tomato chicken) for one of the break fast meals.

NASI MINYAK

Serves 5

INGREDIENTS

2 Tbsp ghee (clarified butter)

1 stick cinnamon

2 cloves

1 star anise

3 green cardamom pods

1 tsp minced ginger

1 tsp minced garlic

150 g basmati rice, washed and drained

300 ml water

1 tsp salt

METHOD

1. In a medium pot, melt ghee over medium heat and fry cinnamon, cloves, star anise and cardamom. Add ginger and garlic, then continue frying until fragrant, about 3 minutes.

2. Add rice, water and salt, then reduce the heat to low. Cover the pot and cook for 20 minutes until the rice is almost cooked. Remove the lid, stir once, then let the rice cook for another 5 minutes uncovered.

3. Turn off the heat and leave to rest for at least 10 minutes before fluffing up the rice and serving. Do not skip this last step or else your rice will be lumpy and wet.

As a child, this was one of my favourite dishes when I was growing up because my mother would cook it when she was introducing me to spicy food. It is spicy, yet sweet, with a slight tinge of sourness coming from the tomatoes in the *rempah* (spice paste). When my mother cooks this dish on regular days, she usually skips the step of frying the chicken separately, opting to simply let the chicken simmer in the *rempah*. My hack for avoiding the tedious frying process is to use the oven's grill setting.

AYAM MASAK MERAH

Serves 5

INGREDIENTS

1 whole chicken, about 1 kg, cut into 12 pieces

2 tsp salt

1 tsp ground turmeric

Vegetable oil as needed

15 dried red chillies, cut, soaked in hot water and drained

1 medium red onion, peeled

5 cloves garlic, peeled

5-cm knob ginger, peeled

1 stick cinnamon

4 cloves

2 star anise

5 green cardamom pods

2 Tbsp chilli sauce

411 g (1 can) diced tomatoes

1 Tbsp sugar

METHOD

1. Prepare chicken pieces by cleaning and patting them dry with paper towels. Place in a large bowl and rub with a teaspoonful of salt, then let them rest for about 30 minutes.

2. In the meantime, preheat the oven to 200°C on the grill setting.

3. Drain excess water and pat chicken pieces dry again. Add ground turmeric and a tablespoonful of oil and mix to coat the chicken well. Arrange on a baking tray and grill for 15–20 minutes. The chicken does not need to be fully cooked, as the grilling here is meant to give it a crispy texture. Set aside.

4. In a blender, blend chillies, onion, garlic and ginger together until a smooth paste forms. You may have to add a dash of water to help in the blending.

5. Heat 3 tablespoonfuls of oil in a heavy-bottomed pot over medium heat. Fry cinnamon, cloves, star anise and cardamom for about a minute. Add blended paste and cook for about 10 minutes over medium-low heat until well tempered, or when the oil starts to separate from the spices.

6. Stir in chilli sauce, diced tomatoes, sugar and the remaining salt. Cook for another 5 minutes before adding the chicken pieces and letting it simmer over low heat for an hour. Serve with *nasi minyak* (see page 26) or white rice.

"During the fasting month, I'll cook *nasi minyak* and serve it with *ayam masak merah* for one of the break fast meals."

Sambal goreng pengantin, or SGP as it is commonly called on the internet, is the true definition of a labour of love. It requires prep work that would take the entire day, from cleaning the ingredients to serving the dish. Then it would probably take less than 20 minutes for you to finish eating the entire pot. Even then, Malay mothers, *makciks* and home cooks still take on the challenge of preparing this dish for major celebrations like Hari Raya. A kilogram each of flank steak, beef lungs and prawns may seem a lot, but SGP is a laborious dish, so it makes no sense to make a small batch. I would halve the recipe, but I do not recommend cooking less than 500 g of each protein. This recipe is definitely not for the amateur, but if you are game for levelling up your kitchen skills, this is it.

SAMBAL GORENG PENGANTIN

Makes 3 kg

INGREDIENTS

Vegetable oil for frying

1 kg flank steak (*daging goreng*), cut into cubes

1 kg beef lungs, boiled and cut into cubes

1 kg prawns, cleaned, peeled and deveined

200 g red chillies, sliced thinly

4 medium red onions, peeled and cut into chunks

2 heads garlic, peeled

60 g ginger, peeled

20 dried red chillies, cut, soaked in hot water and drained

4 candlenuts

5 stalks lemongrass

2 Tbsp cumin seeds

2 Tbsp coriander seeds

2 turmeric leaves

20 kaffir lime leaves

300 g crispy fried shallots

1 litre fresh coconut milk

50 g palm sugar (*gula melaka*)

1 Tbsp brown sugar

1 Tbsp seedless tamarind paste

1–2 tsp salt, or to taste

METHOD

1. In a wok or deep pot, heat enough oil to deep-fry the proteins – flank steak, beef lungs and prawns. While the oil is heating up, drain any excess water from the proteins and prepare 3 baking trays lined with paper towels or fitted with wire racks.

2. Once the oil is hot, begin deep-frying the flank steak in batches to avoid overcrowding the wok, then do the same for the beef lungs and prawns. Transfer the cooked beef and prawns to the prepared baking trays. Leave the wok and frying oil as you will be using it later.

3. Place 100 g red chillies in a blender, together with onions, garlic, ginger, dried red chillies, candlenuts and 2 stalks lemongrass. Blend until a smooth paste forms. You may have to add a dash of water to help in the blending. Set aside spice paste.

4. Toast cumin and coriander seeds in a dry frying pan until fragrant. Use a mortar and pestle to pound the toasted spices into a fine powder. You can use a spice blender, but I find the mortar and pestle brings out a more intense flavour.

5. Reheat the oil in the wok – you should have just enough left so that you're not deep-frying the aromatics. Add blended paste and fry over medium-low heat for 15–20 minutes, until the oil starts to separate from the spices. This process of *pecah minyak* (breaking the oil) is very important in eliminating the raw taste of the aromatics. Add ground spices, turmeric and lime leaves and the remaining lemongrass. Stir in the remaining red chillies and fry for about 5 minutes until the chillies are wilted. Fry for another 10 minutes before adding the proteins and fried shallots, followed by the coconut milk.

6. Mix carefully to make sure every bit of the proteins get covered with the *rempah* (spice paste) and coconut milk. Stir in both sugars, reduce the heat to low, then cover the wok with a lid. Leave this to cook for 1–2 hours until the coconut milk is absorbed, occasionally stirring to make sure nothing sticks to the bottom of the wok.

7. Once you have an almost-dry mix in the wok, add tamarind paste and salt, then stir until well combined. Turn off the heat and serve this dish with *lontong* (compressed rice cakes) or rice.

My husband is a man of simple pleasures. When we first hung out with his friends at a popular coffee shop in town, he ordered *nasi goreng kampung* (Malay-style fried rice) together with *teh tarik* (pulled milk tea). When we had just gotten married, I asked him what he usually has for lunch at work, and he said it was *nasi goreng*. Every other time I'm unable to pack a lunch for him, he would have *nasi goreng* from the canteen at work. Whenever I ask him what he wants to take to work, it would undoubtedly be *nasi goreng*. My husband would probably be an ambassador for this dish if he had not married me. This is a quick recipe I whip up in the mornings for him to take to work on my lazy days.

NASI GORENG KAMPUNG

Serves 4

INGREDIENTS

4 Tbsp peanut oil

2 Tbsp dried anchovies (*ikan bilis*)

1 egg, beaten

5 shallots, peeled

2 cloves garlic, peeled

2.5-cm knob ginger, peeled

1/2 tsp dried prawn paste (*belacan*)

2 Tbsp peeled prawns or fish balls, cooked and sliced into halves

2 Tbsp frozen mixed vegetables

3 cups cooked white rice

2 green chillies, very thinly sliced

1/2 tsp fine sea salt

1/4 tsp ground black pepper

GARNISHING & SERVING

2 Tbsp crispy fried shallots

1 spring onion, finely chopped

1/2 Japanese cucumber, thinly sliced

2 tomatoes, cut into wedges

Sunny side up eggs

Fish crackers (*keropok ikan*)

Sambal belacan (dried prawn paste sambal)

METHOD

1. Heat oil in a wok over medium heat. Once the oil is hot, fry dried anchovies until golden brown, then set aside on a plate lined with paper towels. In the same wok, pour in egg and scramble it using a wooden spoon. Once cooked, set aside together with the anchovies.

2. Place shallots, garlic and ginger in a food processor and blend into a paste. You may have to add a dash of water to help in the blending. In the same wok as before, add dried prawn paste and fry for about a minute on high heat. Add spice paste and sauté for about 2 minutes on high heat.

3. Reduce the heat to medium and add prawns or fish balls, together with mixed vegetables and rice. Return the heat to high and toss the ingredients, making sure the rice is well coated with the spice paste. Do this for about 2 minutes before turning the heat to medium and adding the anchovies and scrambled eggs, along with salt and pepper. Toss all the ingredients together again.

4. Transfer the fried rice onto plates and garnish with fried shallots and spring onion. Serve together with cucumber slices, tomato wedges, sunny side up eggs, fish crackers and *sambal belacan*.

I attended a kindergarten at a local mosque near my childhood home instead of the public kindergartens, which my friends went to. One of my best memories of going to school was the makeshift canteen stall selling traditional *kuih*, snacks and treats. As a six-year-old, I got excited when my mum would let me choose my after-school snack. Sometimes it would be french fries doused in bottled chilli sauce, other times it would be fried doughnuts. One of my favourite after-school snacks was of course, *macaroni goreng* (stir-fried macaroni). It's the perfect marriage of East and West — using pasta instead of noodles as a base for a spicy dry sauce.

MACARONI GORENG

Serves 5

INGREDIENTS

1 tsp cumin seeds
1 tsp coriander seeds
1 medium red onion, peeled and cut into chunks
2 shallots, peeled
3 cloves garlic, peeled
2.5-cm knob ginger, peeled
3 Tbsp vegetable oil
Salt as needed
500 g elbow pasta
1 Tbsp dried chilli paste
200 g minced beef
1 Tbsp tomato paste
1 Tbsp sweet soy sauce (*kicap manis*)

GARNISHING

2 eggs, beaten
Spring onions, chopped
Chinese celery, chopped
Crispy fried shallots

METHOD

1. Toast cumin and coriander seeds in a dry frying pan. Place toasted spices in a blender, together with onion, shallots, garlic, ginger and oil. Blend until a fine paste forms. You may have to add a dash of water if the paste is too thick but not as fine.

2. Boil a pot of water and salt it liberally. Once the water is boiling, add pasta and cook for about 10 minutes, or until al dente, then drain and set aside. Cooking the pasta in salted water ensures that the pasta absorbs the flavours of the *rempah* (spice paste) when it's being fried later on.

3. In the meantime, heat a wok over medium heat and sauté the spice paste until it is tempered, or when the oil starts to separate from the spices. This would take 6–7 minutes with constant stirring. This process of *pecah minyak* (breaking the oil) is very important in eliminating the raw taste of the aromatics. Add chilli paste and continue cooking for another 2–3 minutes.

4. Add minced beef and cook for about 3 minutes on high heat, stirring constantly. Turn the heat to low, then add tomato paste, sweet soy sauce and pasta. Bring the heat back up to high, then toss the pasta and sauce together until well combined. Transfer to a serving dish.

5. Drizzle some oil into a frying pan over medium heat and swirl the pan around to coat its base well. Add eggs, then swirl the pan around to spread the eggs evenly. Cook on one side for about 3 minutes before flipping the omelette and cooking for another minute. Set aside to cool before cutting into strips for garnishing.

6. Serve the pasta garnished with omelette strips, spring onions and Chinese celery, along with fried shallots.

In Singapore *bubur masjid* is always distributed at local mosques during Ramadhan, the fasting month in the Muslim calendar. It is a savoury porridge cooked with a mix of flavourful spices and aromatics, chunks of beef and a hint of coconut milk to make it richer and more decadent. As with any other traditional Malay dishes, the spices and herbs need to be sautéed and tempered with oil for quite a while before adding any other ingredients.

BUBUR MASJID

Serves 4

INGREDIENTS

200 g beef chuck, cubed

1.3 litres water

1 tsp cumin seeds

1 tsp coriander seeds

1/2 tsp black peppercorns

1 big red onion, peeled

8 cloves garlic, peeled

2.5-cm knob ginger, peeled

1 stalk lemongrass, white part only

1/2 tsp ground turmeric

3 Tbsp vegetable oil

1 Tbsp ghee (clarified butter)

1 stick cinnamon

3 green cardamom pods

1 star anise

5 cloves

1 packet *sup bunjut Adabi* (a mix consisting of coriander seeds, aniseed, black peppercorns, cinnamon, star anise, cloves, cardamom)

200 g jasmine rice, washed and drained

150 g canned sweet corn

150 g canned green peas

200 g coconut milk

1 tsp salt

GARNISHING

2 eggs

Spring onions, chopped

Coriander sprigs, chopped

Crispy fried shallots

METHOD

1. Prepare beef by simmering it in 400 ml water over low heat for 30–40 minutes. You can use any cut of beef you prefer, but I quite like beef chuck or tendon for this dish. It gives a nice bite to the porridge's otherwise mushy texture. Set aside the beef and its cooking water as you will need it for the porridge.

2. Toast cumin and coriander seeds with black peppercorns in a dry frying pan. If you have a toaster oven, you can make your life easier by chucking the spices in it for about 2 minutes. Place toasted spices in a food processor, together with onion, garlic, ginger, lemongrass, turmeric and vegetable oil. Blend until a nice, thick paste forms. You may have to add a dash of water to help in the blending.

3. Heat ghee in a large heavy-bottomed pot and add blended spice paste. Do not add any more oil as it has already been added to the spice paste. Sauté for a few minutes, stirring constantly to make sure nothing sticks to the bottom of the pot. Once the spice paste is fragrant, stir in cinnamon, cardamom, star anise, cloves and *sup bunjut*, then cook for about 2 minutes.

4. Add rice, beef and its reserved water, canned vegetables, as well as the remaining 900 ml water and coconut milk to the pot. Stir continuously for about 5 minutes, then turn the heat to low. Cover the pot and let porridge cook gently for about an hour. Season with salt and stir, then cook for another 20–30 minutes.

5. Meanwhile, drizzle some oil into a frying pan. Beat eggs in a separate bowl before pouring into the pan. Swirl the pan around to spread the eggs evenly. Once the edges start to brown and the eggs are somewhat set, use a spatula to gently flip the omelette and cook for another minute. Set aside to cool before cutting into strips for garnishing.

6. Serve the porridge warm or hot and garnish with omelette strips, spring onions and coriander, along with fried shallots.

There is something about this stir-fried rice noodle dish that gets me excited. Whenever I head over to East Coast Food Centre, *kway teow goreng*, or KTG as it is lovingly called on social media, is one of my favourite dishes to order. Apart from the mandatory satay and barbecue chicken wings, KTG makes my Sundays by the beach as *lepak* (chill) as it can be.

KWAY TEOW GORENG

Serves 8

INGREDIENTS

5 Tbsp vegetable oil

2 eggs, beaten

4 heaping Tbsp minced onion

5 cloves garlic, peeled and minced

2.5-cm knob ginger, peeled and minced

2 Tbsp dried chilli paste

4 Tbsp sweet soy sauce (*kicap manis*)

4 Tbsp oyster sauce

200 g chicken breast, sliced thinly

2 squids, cleaned, skinned and sliced into rings

1 fish cake, sliced thinly

800 g fresh flat rice noodles (*kway teow*)

A handful of Chinese chives (*koo chye*), sliced into 2.5-cm lengths

METHOD

1. Heat a large wok with 2 tablespoonfuls of oil, then lower the heat to medium once the oil is hot. Pour in eggs and stir quickly to scramble them as they cook. Set the cooked eggs aside.

2. In the same wok, add the remaining oil and fry minced onion, garlic and ginger together until fragrant. Add chilli paste, soy sauce and oyster sauce. Stir in quickly and bring the heat up to high before adding the chicken slices. Cook for 2–3 minutes.

3. Add squid, fish cake and noodles. Stir-fry all the ingredients until well combined, stirring fast and being careful not to cut up the noodles too much. Cook for 3–4 minutes before adding Chinese chives and eggs, mixing them in well. Serve hot.

This was my first recipe in the *Masterchef Singapore* kitchen as a semi-finalist back in 2018. The judges challenged us to create a dish that represented Chinese cuisine and I presented this to them. This dish was chosen to be in the top three that night, and I nearly won that challenge. You cannot go wrong with a fried chicken recipe. I made my own *mantou* (Chinese buns) for that challenge but please, by all means, make your life easier by getting them off the shelf.

HAR CHEONG GAI MANTOU

Serves 5

INGREDIENTS

2 chicken thighs, boneless

1 Tbsp fermented prawn paste (*har cheong*)

1 tsp dark soy sauce

1 tsp light soy sauce

3 cloves garlic, peeled and chopped

2.5 cm knob ginger, peeled and chopped

100 g all-purpose flour

20 g cornflour

1 tsp baking powder

1 tsp salt

Vegetable oil for deep-frying

PICKLED VEGETABLES

250 ml apple cider vinegar

1 tsp mustard seeds

1 small carrot, peeled and julienned

1 Japanese cucumber, julienned

ASSEMBLY

5 plain *mantou* (Chinese buns), steamed

Sweet Thai chilli sauce for serving

METHOD

1. Prepare the pickled vegetables first by boiling apple cider vinegar with mustard seeds. Once the mixture is boiling, add carrot and cucumber, then turn off the heat. Set aside and allow vegetables to cool.

2. Clean and pat dry chicken, then place in a bowl together with prawn paste, both soy sauces, garlic and ginger. Mix well and leave to marinate for at least an hour or overnight in the refrigerator.

3. Before frying the chicken, combine flour, cornflour, baking powder and salt in a bowl. Heat enough oil for deep-frying in a deep pan or pot over medium heat. Once the oil is hot, coat marinated chicken in flour mixture on both sides and fry for about 5 minutes on each side.

4. Transfer fried chicken to a cooling rack fitted on a baking tray to allow excess oil to drain off.

5. Cut chicken thighs into strips and make a slit in each bun. Divide chicken equally between the buns, top them off with pickled vegetables and serve with Thai chilli sauce on the side.

#weeknightwinners

A hearty lasagna reminds me of the time my Kak Nai became obsessed with making lasagna upon returning from her studies in the UK. She made everything from scratch, save for the pasta sheets. When she got married and moved out of the family home, I missed the lasagna so much, I kept trying to make it. I got away with using instant pasta sauces, but eventually got around to making my own bolognese and béchamel sauces. I remember giving her some to try, and my then 8-year-old niece, who had previously refused to eat lasagna, asked for more of it. I take full credit for getting her to eat lasagna.

KAK NAI'S COPYCAT BEEF LASAGNA

Serves 8

INGREDIENTS

LASAGNA SHEETS

300 g Tipo 00 flour

3 large eggs

1 tsp salt

BÉCHAMEL

80 g unsalted butter

2 cloves garlic, peeled and minced

50 g all-purpose flour

500 ml full-fat milk

100 g mozzarella cheese, grated

100 g cheddar cheese, grated

A pinch of ground nutmeg

ASSEMBLY

500 g bolognese sauce (page 64)

200 g mozzarella cheese, grated

200 g cheddar cheese, grated

50 g parmesan cheese, grated

METHOD

1. Prepare the lasagna sheets by mixing everything in a food processor to form a dough. Tip the crumbly dough into a bowl and knead for a bit until it comes together and firms up nicely. Cover with cling film and leave to rest for 30 minutes before dividing the dough into 5 equal portions. Roll each portion into a ball, place on a tray and cover with a damp cloth until needed.

2. To prepare the béchamel, melt butter in a medium pot over medium heat and fry garlic until fragrant. Turn the heat to medium-low, then add flour and stir quickly to make sure the roux is cooked properly. Stir in milk gradually, allowing it to absorb the roux and thicken up, then add cheeses and nutmeg. Once the béchamel coats the back of a wooden spoon or spatula, remove from the heat.

3. Preheat the oven to 180°C.

4. Roll each dough ball out into a sheet the size of your casserole dish. Each sheet should be opaque but not too thin. Check by holding the lasagna sheet against the light; you should be able to see the shadow of your palm.

5. To assemble the lasagna, spread about a tablespoonful of bolognese sauce over the base of the casserole. Cover with a lasagna sheet, then spoon a quarter of the bolognese sauce over, followed by a fifth of the béchamel and finally a quarter of the mozzarella and cheddar cheeses. Make sure each layer is spread evenly. Repeat to use up the bolognese sauce and both cheeses. Finish with the final lasagna sheet and the remaining béchamel, then top it off with parmesan cheese. This will give you a nice golden crispy crust.

6. Bake for 30-45 minutes, until the cheeses have melted and the top most layer is a beautiful golden brown with spots of dark brown. Remove from the oven and let the lasagna rest for 20-30 minutes before cutting into slices and serving.

Mac 'n' cheese was one of the first few dishes I taught myself to cook, mainly because it's such a comforting and rich dish, and it's difficult to find a good one. Moreover, it's something you can eat while watching TV, or when you're getting over a break-up. This recipe is so simple and fuss free, it can also make a great dinner to whip up after a long day at work. You may add other types of cheeses or other proteins of your choice to this, and it's a great recipe for getting rid of bits and pieces of leftover ingredients too!

MAC 'N' CHEESE

Serves 4

INGREDIENTS

Salt as needed

300 g elbow pasta

2 Tbsp unsalted butter

1 Tbsp all-purpose flour

200 ml milk

1 chicken stock cube

150 g grated cheddar cheese

Ground black pepper, to taste

5 chicken franks, sliced

METHOD

1. Preheat the oven to 180°C.

2. Bring a pot of water to the boil and add a teaspoonful of salt. Cook pasta as per package instructions, then drain and set aside in a baking casserole.

3. In a medium saucepan, melt butter over medium heat. As it melts, add flour and stir quickly to make sure the roux is cooked properly. Stir in milk gradually, then add chicken stock cube and half of the cheese. Whisk until everything is well-combined. Season with salt and pepper.

4. When the cheese sauce starts to thicken, turn off the heat and pour over the pasta. Add sausages and use a fork to mix everything together, ensuring the pasta is well coated with the sauce.

5. Top with the remaining cheese and bake for 30 minutes, or until the top is golden brown. Serve hot.

If there's one type of fish I don't mind splurging on, it certainly is salmon. It is rich and fatty, and it keeps you full for longer. Plus I really do love crispy salmon skin. For this recipe, however, you'll want to keep the salmon skin soaked in the creamy goodness of the sauce. It adds another dimension to the sauce, which makes you want to lick it off the plate.

CREAMY SALMON

Serves 2

INGREDIENTS

2 Tbsp olive oil

300 g salmon fillet, cut into halves lengthwise

2 Tbsp unsalted butter

5 cloves garlic, peeled and chopped

1/2 cup chopped parsley

1/2 cup chopped dill

1 cup heavy cream

Salt, to taste

Freshly cracked black pepper, to taste

METHOD

1. Heat olive oil in a pan over medium heat and cook salmon skin side down for a good 7 minutes. Once the fillets slide around the pan easily, carefully flip them and cook for another 3 minutes. Transfer cooked salmon to a cooling rack to drain off the excess oil.

2. In a saucepan, melt butter over medium heat and fry garlic for about a minute until fragrant. Add the chopped parsley and dill, then quickly stir in cream. Season to taste with salt and pepper and remove from the heat.

3. Place the salmon on serving plates. Pour the sauce over and serve hot. This is best eaten on its own or with a side of toasted bread.

By now you would have noticed that salmon and pasta are my go-to dishes when I'm rushing for time. On weekdays that I work, I avoid rushing to prepare dinner by having my portioned ingredients defrosting in the refrigerator just before I leave for work. Once I am home, I simply turn on the stove and cook. Za'atar is not something everyone has in their pantry but you can substitute it for other herbs like thyme and rosemary. Otherwise, check out your nearest specialty supermarket and you might find this delicious Middle Eastern herb.

ZA'ATAR CRUSTED SALMON

Serves 2

INGREDIENTS

2 Tbsp dried za'atar
1 tsp white sesame seeds
1 tsp black sesame seeds
1 tsp garlic powder
$1/2$ tsp flaky sea salt
2 salmon fillets
4 Tbsp olive oil

METHOD

1. In a bowl, mix za'atar, both sesame seeds, garlic powder and sea salt together. Clean and pat dry salmon fillets.

2. Heat olive oil in a pan over low heat. While the pan is heating up, coat the skin side of the salmon with the herb mixture. Carefully place salmon skin side down in the pan. Increase the heat to medium-low and cook for a good 8 minutes. Once the salmon comes off the pan easily, flip and cook the other side for another 3 minutes.

3. Remove from the heat and serve with some salad and rice of your choice.

This pasta sauce is an adaptation of Marcella Hazan's famous tomato sauce. I've tweaked it to my liking and made it even more flavourful by blending the onions into the sauce. It is my go-to tomato sauce to keep at the back of my refrigerator and for pizza nights too. It's also a good sauce to have when you want to clear your refrigerator of leftovers. The best thing about this pasta sauce is its versatility — add some sausages and pasta, and you're good for dinner!

BEST PASTA SAUCE

Makes about 1 kg

INGREDIENTS

2 cans peeled tomatoes, about 800 g

2 medium red onions, peeled and cut into chunks

5 cloves garlic, peeled

80 g unsalted butter

Salt, to taste

METHOD

1. In a medium saucepan, cook tomatoes, onions and garlic over medium-low heat for 45 minutes.

2. Turn off the heat and use an immersion blender to purée the sauce. Stir in butter while the sauce is still hot, then season with salt to your liking.

3. Use as a pizza or pasta sauce. If you are planning to keep this, transfer to a jar, leave uncovered for a couple of hours to cool completely before covering and refrigerating. It will last 2 weeks in the refrigerator or up to 3 months in the freezer.

I can live without rice and survive entirely on noodles and potatoes. I tend to reach for those two when I'm rushing for time, or when I'm craving for something comforting. These roasted potatoes are perfect with any grilled meats or fish, and even more delicious with some scrambled eggs. Make it for dinner or breakfast — they are guaranteed to fill you up.

ROASTED POTATOES

Serves 4

INGREDIENTS

500 g russet potatoes
1 litre water for boiling
2 Tbsp salt
2 Tbsp olive oil
4 sprigs fresh rosemary, removed from stem and chopped
Freshly cracked black pepper, to taste
Sea salt, to taste

METHOD

1. Preheat the oven to 200°C on the grill setting.

2. It is important that you use russet potatoes to get fluffy insides and crispy outsides. Waxy potatoes do no justice to roasted potatoes. Clean and drain potatoes, then cut into chunks.

3. In a big pot, place potatoes, water and salt. Do not be afraid of the amount of salt at this stage. The potatoes need to be salted while they are parboiled to ensure a depth of flavour when they are roasted. Bring the pot of potatoes to the boil, then boil for 4-6 minutes. When a fork stuck into a piece comes off easily, remove potatoes from the heat.

4. Drain potatoes in a colander, shaking off as much excess water as possible. Using a fork, gently fluff the potatoes by tossing them around. The bruised parts will create a crisp texture when roasting.

5. Transfer to a roasting tray and drizzle olive oil all over the potatoes. Add rosemary, black pepper and salt, then use the same fork to toss and make sure each piece of potato gets coated in the seasoning. Grill for 20 minutes, then remove from the oven to flip and toss the potatoes around in the tray. The hot oil will help you achieve that delicious crispy potato skin.

6. Return to the oven and grill for another 10-15 minutes. Serve hot as a side dish or on its own.

Some days when I crave for rice, I want a flavourful and simple rice dish that I can eat with some grilled or roast meat. Herbed rice is a great way to get rid of leftover herbs you have at the back of your refrigerator (we are all guilty of that), and a perfect alternative to fried rice, which takes too much effort sometimes.

HERBED RICE

Serves 3

INGREDIENTS

1 cup basmati rice
2 Tbsp unsalted butter
2 cloves
3 green cardamom pods
1 stick cinnamon
2 cups water
1 Tbsp chopped coriander
1 Tbsp chopped parsley
3 Tbsp cashew nuts, fried or oven roasted
Crispy fried shallots for garnishing

METHOD

1. Rinse and drain your rice, then set aside.

2. In a medium saucepan over medium heat, melt butter. Add cloves, cardamom pods and cinnamon, then sauté until fragrant, about 1–2 minutes.

3. Add the rice and water. You can check that the amount of water is right by sticking your index finger into the pot to touch the top of the rice, and making sure the water level reaches the first joint of your finger. Stir well, then cover the pot and cook for 20–25 minutes on medium-low heat until water is fully absorbed and rice is cooked.

4. Stir the cooked rice once using a spoon and leave uncovered. Do not touch the rice any more at this point. Allow it to cool for 10 minutes before adding the chopped herbs.

5. To serve, garnish with cashew nuts and fried shallots.

Rainy days are best for some comforting porridge, or in this case, some congee made with leftover rice. It's a fast meal that requires almost no cooking and uses pantry staples you would already have. There were times I've ordered congee at local dim sum places only to be left disappointed, so this is certainly one of a few dishes I would rather make at home.

CHINESE-STYLE CONGEE

Serves 2

INGREDIENTS

3 cups water

$\frac{1}{2}$ chicken stock cube

3-cm knob ginger, peeled and julienned

2 cups leftover rice

1 tsp salt

1 century egg

$\frac{1}{2}$ can braised peanuts, about 85 g

1 bird's eye chilli (*cili padi*), thinly sliced

Light soy sauce, to taste

METHOD

1. In a medium pot, place water, stock cube and ginger. Bring to the boil over medium heat, then add rice and salt. Reduce the heat to low and let simmer for 10–15 minutes.

2. Turn off the heat and let congee rest for 5 minutes before serving. Serve with a century egg cut into wedges, braised peanuts, bird's eye chilli and soy sauce.

This is probably one of the easiest and my favourite pasta sauce to make. I usually make a big batch and store the leftovers in the refrigerator for days on which I'm too lazy to cook something from scratch. This bolognese sauce is also great for lasagnas, especially when paired with my homemade béchamel (see page 46). The secret to making a delicious bolognese is to let it stew for a few hours, sometimes up to 4 hours on low heat. The addition of some blackcurrant cordial (I use Ribena) also helps to cut through the acidity of the tomatoes, which some might find too overwhelming.

BOLOGNESE SAUCE

Serves 4

INGREDIENTS

2 Tbsp olive oil

2 medium yellow onions, peeled and diced

5 cloves garlic, peeled and minced

1 kg minced beef

1 beef stock cube

2 cans pomodoro tomatoes, about 800 g

1 Tbsp tomato paste

100 ml blackcurrant cordial or grape juice

3 sprigs fresh rosemary, stems removed, or 2 Tbsp dried rosemary

1 tsp dried marjoram

1 tsp dried sage

2 tsp dried basil

Salt, to taste

Ground black pepper, to taste

METHOD

1. Drizzle olive oil in a heavy-bottomed pot over medium heat. Olive oil heats up relatively quickly, so once bubbles appear when you place a wooden spoon in the oil, add onions and sauté until fragrant and translucent, stirring continuously to make sure onions do not burn.

2. Stir in garlic quickly and reduce the heat to low (garlic burns easily). After 1–2 minutes, add minced beef and mix well with the aromatics, cooking until the meat is browned. Browning the beef well gets you a tastier and more flavourful bolognese sauce.

3. Add stock cube, tomatoes, tomato paste, blackcurrant cordial and herbs. Stir to mix everything well before reducing the heat to low. Season with salt and pepper to your liking, then cover the pot. Simmer on low heat for at least 2–3 hours for best results.

4. I only serve my bolognese with either pappardelle or fettuccine pasta, so that the pasta scoops up the chunks of meat as I dig into it. Set aside any leftover sauce in the refrigerator for a wonderful lasagna too.

I was 23 years old when I first travelled on my own. I headed to Morocco, and then to Europe, for a month-long soul-searching journey. A friend of mine was on a student exchange programme in Casablanca, the capital of Morocco, so I took the opportunity to stay with her and travel to a few cities on my own. When I got to Fez after a long bus trip, I ordered some food from the backpacker hostel's kitchen and I was pleasantly surprised by the lamb stew. The meat was fresh, tender and the combination of spices made a happy little dance in my mouth. I soon found out that the secret ingredient of dried apricots completed the holy trinity of spicy, salty and sweet.

MOROCCAN LAMB STEW WITH COUSCOUS

Serves 5

INGREDIENTS

HARISSA SPICE MIX

1 tsp ground coriander

1 tsp ground turmeric

1 tsp ground cumin

1 tsp ground ginger

1/2 tsp smoked paprika powder

1 tsp ground caraway seeds

COUSCOUS

300 ml boiling water

2 cups couscous

2 Tbsp unsalted butter

Salt, to taste

Celery leaves for garnishing

LAMB STEW

2 Tbsp all-purpose flour

2 tsp salt

1 tsp ground black pepper

1 kg lamb chuck roast, cubed and trimmed

2 Tbsp olive oil

4 cloves garlic, peeled and chopped

2.5-cm knob ginger, peeled and minced

500 ml water

1 chicken stock cube

5 tomatoes, cut into chunks

2 large carrots, sliced

1 cup dried apricots, coarsely chopped

METHOD

1. In a small bowl, combine all the spices for the spice mix. Set aside.

2. To make the lamb stew, combine flour, salt and pepper on a plate and mix well. Gently coat lamb cubes on all sides with flour mixture. In the meantime, heat oil over medium heat in a Dutch oven or a heavy-bottomed pot and brown the lamb cubes in batches. If the pot is overcrowded, the lamb might not brown evenly or end up getting boiled. Set aside the browned lamb on a dripping tray.

3. Using the same pot, add garlic, ginger, water and stock cube. Stir to dissolve the stock cube before adding tomatoes and bringing to the boil. Once the mixture is boiling, reduce the heat to low and carefully add the lamb pieces to the pot, followed by the spice mix. Cover and let simmer over a gentle heat for about 1.5 hours.

4. Uncover the pot, add carrots, along with the dried apricots, and stir gently. Cover again and cook for another 15 minutes, or until the carrots are fork tender.

5. Meanwhile, mix boiling water with couscous and let sit until all the water has been absorbed. Mix in butter and salt, then gently fluff up couscous with a fork. Serve the lamb stew with couscous and garnish with celery leaves.

While we were dating, my husband Faeez knew that I love to cook and would drop subtle hints about what his favourite foods were by asking if I knew how to cook certain dishes. This butter chicken was one of the first few dishes I cooked for him just after our engagement. Needless to say, whenever he's craving for butter chicken, he would come up to me and say, "Remember the time you made me butter chicken before we got married?" This recipe is perfect with some home-made naan (see page 97).

THE BEST BUTTER CHICKEN

Serves 5

INGREDIENTS

2 boneless chicken thighs
Salt as needed
$1/2$ tsp coriander seeds
$1/2$ tsp cumin seeds
5-cm knob ginger, peeled
10 cloves garlic, peeled
3 green chillies
120 ml Greek yoghurt
$1/2$ tsp Kashmiri red chilli powder
A pinch of saffron

BUTTER CHICKEN GRAVY

1 tsp vegetable oil
2 Tbsp unsalted butter
1 stick cinnamon
4 green cardamom pods
2 cloves
1 red onion, peeled and chopped
4 Tbsp canned chopped tomatoes
2 Tbsp tomato paste

1 Tbsp Kashmiri red chilli powder
1 Tbsp ground coriander
250 ml heavy cream
1 tsp fenugreek leaves (*kasuri methi*)

1 tsp honey
Juice of $1/2$ lemon
Salt to taste
$1/2$ cup chopped coriander leaves

METHOD

1. Cut chicken thighs into 2.5-cm pieces and place in a medium bowl. Add about a tablespoonful of salt and mix well using your hands. Set aside for at least 30 minutes.

2. In the meantime, toast coriander and cumin seeds in a dry frying pan. Use a mortar and pestle to pound the toasted spices into a fine powder. (Alternatively, use pre-ground cumin and coriander, but use a tad more for each.)

3. Blend ginger, garlic and chillies together to form a fine paste. Set aside 2 tablespoonfuls for the gravy. Add the remaining paste to the chicken, along with the ground spices, Greek yoghurt, chilli powder and saffron. Mix well and leave to marinate for at least 2 hours.

4. Preheat the oven to 200°C on the grill setting. Arrange chicken pieces on a baking tray and grill for 20-30 minutes until cooked. The chicken should be charred a little to mimic a barbecue flavour.

5. To make the gravy, heat oil and butter in a heavy-bottomed pot over medium heat. Add cinnamon, cardamom and cloves, then cook for about a minute until fragrant. Add onion and reserved ginger-garlic-chilli paste, cooking for another 3 minutes before adding chopped tomatoes, tomato paste, chilli powder, ground coriander and heavy cream. Let simmer for about 3 minutes over low heat.

6. Turn off the heat and fish out the cinnamon stick. Use an immersion blender to puree the mixture into a smooth gravy. Stir in fenugreek leaves, honey and lemon juice. Season with salt to taste.

7. To serve, place grilled chicken in a bowl and pour gravy over it. Garnish with chopped coriander leaves. This is best served with naan or plain basmati rice.

#easyentertaining

I love exploring new foods and cooking techniques. My YouTube feed features mostly recipe videos, while my Instagram feed is filled with beautiful pictures of food. I try not to jump on trends, but I'll give them a try to see what the hype is about. This beetroot hummus was something I tasted while attending a vegan cooking class — yes, this carnivore went for a vegan cooking class. I tweaked the recipe a little to make it taste more similar to regular hummus. Make this in a large batch and store it in the refrigerator if you like snacking and don't want to feel guilty about it.

BEETROOT HUMMUS

Serves 4

INGREDIENTS

2 cloves garlic, peeled

200 g canned chickpeas, rinsed and drained

60 ml water

2 Tbsp lemon juice

200 g cooked beetroot

6 Tbsp extra virgin olive oil, plus extra for serving

4 Tbsp toasted sesame seeds or tahini paste

½ tsp fine sea salt

Ground paprika for serving

METHOD

1. Place garlic, chickpeas, water, lemon juice, beetroot, olive oil, toasted sesame seeds and sea salt in a food processor and blitz for 3–4 minutes until a fine and smooth paste forms.

2. Spoon hummus onto a plate, sprinkle with paprika and drizzle with more olive oil. Serve with warm pita bread or celery sticks on the side.

On days I have too much leftover roast chicken, pieces of cold cuts or wilting vegetables crying out to me to be eaten, I make this one-pot baked pasta that's fast, easy and pretty satisfying. Use whatever ingredients you have at hand and adjust the quantity of cheeses to your liking.

BAKED PASTA

Serves 5

INGREDIENTS

200 g chicken breast

Salt as needed

200 g penne pasta

1 Tbsp smoked paprika

1 Tbsp olive oil

2 Tbsp unsalted butter

5 cloves garlic, peeled and minced

100 ml heavy cream

100 g mozzarella cheese, grated

Ground black pepper to taste

100 g broccoli, cleaned and cut into chunks

METHOD

1. Preheat the oven to 200°C.

2. Clean chicken breast and cut into cubes, then rub a teaspoonful of salt all over and let stand for about 10 minutes to extract excess water.

3. Meanwhile, cook pasta as per package instructions. Remember to salt the water for the pasta so that the final dish would not be bland. Drain and toss the cooked pasta in a colander and set aside.

4. Drain and pat dry chicken before rubbing with smoked paprika. Heat olive oil in a medium pan over medium heat. Once the oil is hot, add chicken pieces and cook until browned and cooked through. Set aside the chicken pieces, reserving the oil in the pan.

5. To the same pan, add butter and garlic. Fry garlic for about 2 minutes over medium heat until the butter is melted. Gradually add cream and half of the cheese, stirring constantly to make sure the white sauce does not split or over boil. Once the sauce is smooth, season with salt and pepper to taste, then remove from the heat.

6. Combine pasta, chicken pieces, broccoli and white sauce in a 30 x 20-cm (12 x 8-in) casserole dish. Using a pair of tongs, toss everything together until well mixed, then top with the remaining cheese. Bake for 20 minutes until the top is golden brown and crusty.

7. Serve hot or warm, however you prefer it. You can add more vegetables and meat, or use a variety of cheeses to make this dish your own. It's an extremely versatile meal for dinner or when guests arrive at the last minute.

On days I feel like eating something light yet filling, I almost always reach for a salad. While it may seem pretentious that I, a foodie, find salads comforting, the truth is it also allows me more room to binge on the next meal. It's all about making the calories count, after all. However, a caprese salad is full of creamy mozzarella goodness, so nothing about this is as healthy as you want it to be.

CAPRESE SALAD

Serves 3

INGREDIENTS

1 ball fresh mozzarella cheese, about 125 g

1 big fresh heirloom tomato

10 fresh basil leaves

2 Tbsp balsamic vinegar

2 Tbsp extra virgin olive oil

1 tsp fine sugar

1 tsp salt

Freshly cracked black pepper to taste

METHOD

1. Slice fresh mozzarella and tomato into discs. If you cannot find any heirloom tomatoes, any fresh tomatoes will do too. You can even use cherry or grape tomatoes. The key ingredient not to swap out here is definitely the fresh mozzarella. Arrange alternate slices of tomato and cheese together with the basil on a medium plate.

2. In a small bowl, place balsamic vinegar, oil, sugar, salt and pepper. Whisk the dressing together for 1-2 minutes until the sugar is dissolved. Adjust seasoning to your preference.

3. Drizzle the dressing over the cheese and tomatoes. Serve cold. This is best served as an appetiser, but feel free to double or triple the recipe to make it a meal on its own.

#onthegrill

I neither watch Korean dramas nor listen to K-Pop. But the one thing the Koreans have me at is certainly their food. I love watching recipe videos of Korean food, and I constantly crave spicy soupy dishes often featured on television shows. It doesn't help that many Korean food joints in Singapore are halal-certified, making it easy for me to feed this addiction. Gochujang is a spicy paste of red chilli pepper flakes, fermented soybeans, glutinous rice and salt. Commercial gochujang usually contains alcohol since artificially fermenting the soybeans will quicken the process. Fortunately, halal gochujang is readily available in the market, making it easy for those practising the halal diet to consume Korean foods.

GOCHUJANG GRILLED CHICKEN

Serves 4-5

INGREDIENTS

1 kg chicken wings
1 Tbsp salt
100 ml gochujang sauce
1 Tbsp dark soy sauce
1 Tbsp light soy sauce
1 tsp sesame oil
1 tsp olive oil
Sesame seeds for garnishing

METHOD

1. Clean and pat dry chicken wings. Sprinkle salt over, ensuring that each wing is covered by some salt. Set aside for an hour.

2. Add the remaining ingredients except sesame seeds to the wings and mix to coat every piece well. You can use your hands to do this. Cover and let the marinated wings sit in the refrigerator for at least an hour. You can leave them overnight and grill them the next day too.

3. To cook, preheat the oven to 200°C on the grill setting. Arrange the wings on a tray and grill for 25–35 minutes, until cooked through.

4. Transfer chicken wings to a serving plate and garnish with sesame seeds. Serve as a side dish or eat them as a snack.

Lamb chop is one of my family's favourite meat to grill whenever we have barbecues. It is fast to cook, easy to prep and delicious when cooked well. I've found my go-to lamb chop guy at the local wet market — he cuts the chops almost to perfection for a good price. This recipe calls for balsamic vinegar, which may contain alcohol, so make sure you grab hold of the halal-certified ones. Most of the specialty supermarkets stock them in the health foods section.

HONEY LAMB CHOPS

Serves 3

INGREDIENTS

6 lamb chops

1 tsp freshly cracked black pepper

1 tsp sea salt

60 ml balsamic vinegar

1 Tbsp honey

1 Tbsp Dijon mustard

1 clove garlic, peeled and crushed

3 sprigs fresh rosemary, stems removed, chopped

2 Tbsp olive oil

METHOD

1. In a large bowl, combine all the ingredients except olive oil and use your hands to get the flavours into every nook and cranny of the lamb chops. Leave to marinate for at least an hour.

2. Place a cast iron pan over high heat and add olive oil. Once the pan is hot, fry the lamb chops, cooking for 5-6 minutes on each side. The lamb chops should be a bit charred and blackened. I prefer my lamb to be well done as medium rare lamb sometimes tastes too gamey. Let rest for about 10 minutes before serving with sides of your choosing.

This recipe was an accidental one; while I was at my mum's place, we realised she had not marinated the wings for the next meal. I took the opportunity to ransack her kitchen, just like I used to, and voila! This is an easy dish to serve, especially if you have last-minute guests. This grilled chicken will leave them wanting more, making you wish you had at least five kilos of wings (or whatever chicken parts you're using) in your refrigerator.

KAMPUNG-STYLE GRILLED CHICKEN

Serves 8

INGREDIENTS

1 kg chicken wings, or chicken parts of your choice

2 Tbsp salt

4 Tbsp dried chilli paste

4 Tbsp meat curry powder

1 tsp ground turmeric

2 Tbsp ground coriander

2 Tbsp ground cumin

2 Tbsp vegetable oil

METHOD

1. Clean and pat dry chicken pieces. Rub salt all over the pieces and let sit in the refrigerator for 15–30 minutes. If you are rushing for time, 5 minutes would suffice. Add the remaining ingredients except the oil and mix well, using your hands if you must.

2. Refrigerate chicken for at least an hour or overnight. Preheat the oven to 200°C on the grill setting and prepare a roasting tray. You may use an air fryer for this recipe with a similar setting, though an air fryer would not need preheating.

3. Arrange chicken pieces neatly on the prepared tray and drizzle oil all over. Grill for 20–30 minutes, turning them over midway. Serve on their own or as a side.

During Eid or special occasions, there tends to be leftover gravy from all the delicious festive dishes. One of my favourite gravies to incorporate into a new meal is rendang gravy. All you need is a good piece of steak and some frites to go with it and you'll have a meal in less than 30 minutes.

RENDANG STEAK AND FRITES

Serves 2

INGREDIENTS

250 g wagyu rib-eye steak
Salt as needed
2 medium potatoes
Vegetable oil as needed
Freshly cracked black pepper as needed
4 Tbsp leftover rendang gravy

METHOD

1. Prepare steak by cleaning and patting it dry with paper towels. Rub some salt onto both sides of the steak and let it sit while you prepare the potatoes.

2. Peel and julienne potatoes into 2.5-cm matchsticks. Place potato matchsticks in a bowl of water as you cut them. Wash potatoes in a colander under running tap water, drain and shake off excess water. Transfer potatoes to a baking tray lined with paper towels.

3. Prepare 2 more baking trays lined with paper towels or fitted with wire racks. In a deep pot, heat enough oil for deep-frying over low heat. Once the oil is hot, fry potatoes a handful at a time to avoid overcrowding the pot. Cook for about 4 minutes, then transfer to a prepared baking tray. Drain all the potatoes on the first tray.

4. Increase the heat to medium, then deep-fry the potatoes in batches a second time, this time for 5 minutes each. Drain all the twice-fried potatoes on the second baking tray. Salt as desired while still hot.

5. Heat a cast iron skillet over high heat for about 3 minutes, then reduce the heat to medium-low as you drizzle in 4 tablespoonfuls of oil. Season each side of the steak with freshly cracked black pepper. Once the oil is smoking hot, cook steak for about 4 minutes on one side before flipping and cooking for another 3 minutes. You'll want to cook the steak until medium rare.

6. Rest steak for a good 5 minutes on a cooling rack before slicing. Serve with frites and leftover rendang gravy.

A good old roast chicken is one of my go-to dishes when I'm too lazy to tend to the stove or rushing for time. On weekends when I'm out in the day, I like to make this for dinner by prepping it in the morning, then popping it in the oven when I'm back. One hour of unattended cooking as you rest and shower after a long day out is certainly a great life hack.

SUNDAY ROAST CHICKEN

Serves 4-5

INGREDIENTS

1 whole chicken, about 1-1.2kg

1 tsp salt

5 cloves garlic, crushed and peeled

1 red onion, peeled and cut into quarters

1 Tbsp unsalted butter, softened

2 Tbsp dried Italian herb mix

1 tsp ground black pepper

1 Tbsp olive oil

METHOD

1. Preheat the oven to 170°C on the grill setting.

2. Clean and pat dry chicken. Rub all over with salt and let sit for about 15 minutes before stuffing onion and garlic into its cavity.

3. Mix butter, herb mix and pepper together, then rub the chicken all over with it, especially in between the skin and meat. You'll get crispy skin with moist chicken meat this way.

4. Place chicken on a roasting tray and drizzle olive oil all over just before placing in the oven. Roast for about 45 minutes, then turn the heat up to 200°C and cook for another 15 minutes.

5. Serve warm with a side of potatoes or rice.

Whenever I've travelled to Australia, my friends would hold a barbecue for me with fresh meats, sausages and burger patties that are home-made. Meat was ground at the shop upon ordering, and my friends would season them at home just before placing them on the grill. These patties require almost no prep because wagyu meat has a distinct taste on its own. You can always jazz these burgers up with sauces of your choice.

WAGYU BURGER PATTIES

Makes 8 patties

INGREDIENTS

500 g minced wagyu beef
2 Tbsp dried rosemary
$\frac{1}{2}$ tsp salt
$\frac{1}{2}$ tsp freshly cracked black pepper
Olive oil as needed
8 brioche burger buns (page 95)

METHOD

1. Place beef, rosemary, salt and pepper in a bowl and use your hands to mix until everything is well combined. Divide into 8 equal portions and shape each one into a ball by cupping it with both hands and making sure it is packed tightly. Lightly flatten the patties and place them on a baking sheet. Leave to rest in the refrigerator for at least an hour.

2. Let patties sit at room temperature 30 minutes before grilling them. Lightly grease a cast iron pan with some olive oil and heat over medium heat. Once the oil is hot, cook patties 2 at a time to avoid overcrowding. Cook for 4–5 minutes on each side to make sure patties are medium rare. Set cooked patties aside while you grill the buns.

3. Slice buns into halves, then grill on the same cast iron pan to soak up the flavourful oil from the patties. Cook buns on both sides until slightly charred.

4. Assemble the burgers with vegetables of your choice and any other additions like a sunny side up. Serve warm.

#doughordoughnut

Doughnuts are the best desserts to have because they are small and comforting. It's great for days you're craving a whole load of carbs and sweetness. This recipe is simple enough for you to make with your pantry staples, though feel free to jazz it up with chocolate spreads and sprinkles of your choice, or simply go with a dusting of icing or fine sugar.

DOUGHNUTS

Makes 18 doughnuts

INGREDIENTS

50 g castor sugar

190 ml lukewarm water

1 tsp active dry yeast or 16 g fresh yeast

500 g all-purpose flour, plus more for dusting

3 large eggs

1 tsp lemon zest

100 g unsalted butter, at room temperature

1 tsp salt

Vegetable oil for frying

Powdered sugar for dusting

METHOD

1. In the mixing bowl of a stand mixer, combine sugar, warm water and active dry yeast. Lightly mix using a fork and let stand for about 10 minutes. If you are using fresh yeast, you don't need to let it stand.

2. Add flour, eggs, and lemon zest to the yeast mixture. Using the hook attachment, mix and knead for about 10 minutes until the dough starts coming together. Add butter and salt, then continue kneading for 15-20 minutes until the dough comes off the sides of the mixing bowl or it does not tear in the window pane test. The dough should be glossy and smooth. Cover the bowl with a tea towel and leave to rest for an hour.

3. Dust your countertop or work surface with a bit of flour. Punch down the proofed dough to deflate it, then roll out into a rectangle about 1 cm thick. Using a doughnut-shaped cutter, cut out 18 rings. Place the dough rings on a tray lined with baking paper, keeping plenty of space around each one, then cover with a tea towel. Let rest for an hour before frying. The trimmings can be cut into smaller odd-shaped pieces or balls, covered and left to rest as well.

4. Fill a medium pot with vegetable oil, until about 5 cm deep, and place over medium heat. Once the oil is hot, gently place 4 dough rings in the oil and fry for 3 minutes on each side until golden brown. If the oil is too hot and the doughnuts get a little too brown, lower the heat.

5. Place fried doughnuts on a cooling rack on top of a baking tray. Leave to cool for about 10 minutes before dusting with some powdered sugar, or decorate as you wish by piping some chocolate spread or creamy peanut butter onto them.

I'm a burger snob — and by this I mean I judge a good burger by its buns. I love it when burger places make their own burger buns, and it certainly is best when you make your own at home. Burgers are easy to make, so put in the extra effort to make your own bread to complete a satisfying burger meal.

BRIOCHE BURGER BUNS

Makes 8 buns

INGREDIENTS

20 g castor sugar

80 ml water

150 ml milk

2 tsp dried instant yeast

450 g bread flour

1 egg yolk

1 egg

80 g unsalted butter, cut into cubes, at room temperature

1 tsp salt

Vegetable oil as needed

EGG WASH & TOPPING

1 egg yolk

1 Tbsp milk

1 Tbsp black and white sesame seeds

METHOD

1. In a medium pot, combine sugar, water and milk over low heat until it is warm to touch. Be careful not to overheat this mixture. Add instant yeast and set aside for 10 minutes to allow the yeast to activate.

2. Using a stand mixer with a hook attachment, mix flour, egg yolk, egg and milk mixture together and knead for 10–15 minutes on medium speed. Add butter one cube at a time and knead until incorporated before adding salt. Knead for another 5 minutes.

3. Lightly dust your countertop or work surface with flour and tip the dough onto it. Knead by hand for another 1–2 minutes, then shape the dough into a ball by tucking the dough in and creating a seam. Lightly grease the same mixing bowl with some vegetable oil and place the dough seam side down in it. Cover the bowl and leave to proof for an hour.

4. Tip the proofed dough onto a lightly floured surface, punch down to deflate it, then divide into 8 equal pieces. You may weigh them if you prefer accuracy. Shape each piece into a small ball and place on a lightly floured baking tray. Make sure there is room around each bun to let it double in size. Cover with a tea towel and leave buns to proof for an hour.

5. Preheat the oven to 160°C. Gently whisk egg yolk and milk together, then brush the egg wash over the buns. Sprinkle with sesame seeds and bake for 15–20 minutes until golden brown.

6. Transfer to a wire rack and let the buns cool completely before slicing or eating.

I love bread so much. I love making bread at home even more. I got obsessed with making these naan once I perfected the recipe. I was making them every other week and eating them with chicken curry, butter chicken and rendang, to the point that my husband had to say he had had enough naan to last him the year.

NAAN

Makes 10 pieces

INGREDIENTS

375 g all-purpose flour, plus more for dusting

1 1/2 Tbsp yoghurt

1 Tbsp active dry yeast, or 16 g fresh yeast

1 Tbsp castor sugar

1/2 tsp salt

METHOD

1. In a medium bowl, combine flour, yoghurt, yeast and sugar together and knead for about 10 minutes before adding salt. Continue kneading for another 15 minutes, or until the dough does not tear in the window pane test. Alternatively, combine all the ingredients in a stand mixer's mixing bowl. Using the hook attachment, knead the dough for 15–20 minutes. Cover the bowl with a dry tea towel and leave to rest for an hour.

2. Divide the proofed dough into 10 equal portions and shape into balls. Lightly dust your countertop with flour, then roll each ball into a flat oblong shape using a rolling pin. Keep the dough covered with a damp cloth to prevent it from drying out and roll out each portion just before cooking.

3. Prepare a small bowl of water by the stove. Heat a cast iron pan over medium heat. Once the pan is hot, lightly moisten one side of the rolled dough and gently place the wet side on the pan. Do not attempt to flip the naan until the top has puffed up nicely, about 3–4 minutes. You should be able to flip the naan easily once its bottom has charred. Cook the other side for another 1–2 minutes, then place in a bowl lined with a tea towel.

4. Repeat to cook the remaining dough, then serve with a hot bowl of the best butter chicken (see page 68). Foolproof!

I spent a lot of my childhood with my mum, mainly because she had already left the workforce by the time she had me. I grew up tagging along on trips to the market and watching my mum cook in the kitchen — only watching because she rarely allowed me in the kitchen while she was cooking. I was fascinated by Ibu's patience at handling dough whenever she made roti Boyan (Boyanese stuffed pastry). She would spend at least an hour, sitting down and listening to the morning radio, kneading the dough perfectly until she was satisfied. By lunchtime, the roti Boyan would be ready. I loved it when we had leftovers for me to take to school the next day.

IBU'S ROTI BOYAN

Makes 5 pies

INGREDIENTS

500 g all-purpose flour
1 tsp salt
300 ml warm water (plus more if need be)
20 g unsalted butter, softened to room temperature
Vegetable oil as needed

FILLING

5 medium waxy potatoes (you could use russet too)
5 eggs
100 g Chinese parsley, chopped
100 g spring onions, chopped
1 tsp salt
1 tsp ground white pepper

METHOD

1. In a large mixing bowl, combine flour and salt. Add 2 tablespoonfuls of water at a time and knead until the dough comes together. Do not be alarmed if it's too sticky. Add butter and knead until well incorporated. If the dough is too sticky, add a bit more flour, but ensure that the dough stays soft throughout the entire kneading process. Alternatively, you can place everything in a stand mixer's mixing bowl and let the machine do the hard work. Once the dough has come together nicely and appears smooth, form it into a ball, cover the bowl with a dry tea towel and leave to rest for an hour.

2. Peel and cut potatoes into chunks and add to a pot filled with water. Bring to the boil and cook until a fork used to gently poke the potatoes slides out easily. Drain and return potatoes to the same pot. In a separate bowl, crack eggs and beat until fluffy and well combined. Mash the potatoes before adding eggs, parsley, spring onions, salt and pepper. Mix until well combined, then set aside.

3. Grease 2 serving plates about the size of your palm with vegetable oil and lightly dust your countertop or work surface with flour. Divide the proofed dough into 10 equal portions. You may weigh them if you prefer accuracy or just eyeball it if you're lazy like me. Keep the rest of the dough covered with a cloth while you are working on a portion.

4. Roll out a portion of dough to the size of a serving plate, frequently turning the dough while rolling it out to prevent sticking. Place it on an oiled serving plate and stretch it out as much as possible so that it is the size of the plate, then add a cup of filling to its centre. Roll out a second portion of dough and carefully place it over the filling. Press the 2 layers of dough together so that they stick, then crimp the sides like you would for curry puffs, pinching the edges together and folding them in at an angle to get a ridge. Repeat this process for the remaining dough and filling.

5. Heat a teaspoonful of oil in a non-stick pan over medium-low heat. Slowly slide a pie onto the pan and cook for 3 minutes on each side. If you wish to freeze and keep the pies, this is where you remove it from the heat and let cool before freezing. If serving or consuming immediately, continue cooking each side for another 5 minutes over low heat, or until the crust has a nice deep brown colour.

6. Serve with *sambal tumis* (page 19).

For a period of time, my Instagram feed was flooded with people either selling cinnamon rolls or trying to bake them on their own. Cinnamon is a somewhat acquired taste and not many people I know enjoy them unless they are truly foodies. I have found a way to keep the cinnamon taste subtle, while adding a flavour that will keep the picky eaters satiated.

CINNAMON ROLLS

Makes 12 rolls

INGREDIENTS

DOUGH

115 ml milk

2 eggs

8 g fresh yeast

50 g castor sugar

45 g unsalted butter, chilled

322 g all-purpose flour, plus more for dusting

3 g salt

FILLING

50 g dark brown sugar

50 g brown sugar

5 g ground cinnamon

5 g ground nutmeg

40 g unsalted butter, at room temperature

CREAM CHEESE GLAZE

85 g cream cheese

40 g castor sugar

25 g milk

5 g vanilla bean paste or flavouring

METHOD

1. Heat milk in a saucepan over low heat for about 5 minutes. The milk should be lukewarm – if you dip a finger in, it should not scald you. Remove from the heat and lightly whisk in eggs, yeast and sugar.

2. In a stand mixer's mixing bowl, use your fingertips to rub butter into flour to create a sandy mixture resembling breadcrumbs. Using the hook attachment on the lowest speed, begin kneading the mixture. Gradually add the milk mixture, increasing the speed gradually as the dough comes together. Knead on medium speed for about 8 minutes, then add salt. Continue kneading until the dough does not tear in the window pane test or it starts to come off the sides of the mixing bowl.

3. Lightly dust your countertop or work surface with flour and tip the dough onto it. Be sure to remove any dough from the hook attachment. Using your hands, knead the dough for about 3 minutes before shaping into a ball. Lightly grease the same mixing bowl with some vegetable oil and place the dough seam side down in it. Cover and leave to rest for about an hour before shaping.

4. Meanwhile, prepare the filling by whisking together both sugars and ground spices.

5. Punch down the proofed dough, then tip onto a lightly floured work surface and roll out into a 30 x 15-cm (12 x 6-in) rectangle. Spread generously with butter, then sprinkle the sugar-spice mixture on top, making sure to use up both ingredients.

6. From the longer end closer to you, carefully roll up the dough tightly. Move from right to left, then left to right, so the dough rolls up nicely. Cut the log into 12 equal pieces, each about 2.5 cm thick. Grease a 20-cm (8-in) round baking pan or cast iron skillet with butter. Arrange the rolls on the pan, leaving a small space around each one.

7. Leave the rolls to rest for about an hour until roughly doubled in size. Halfway through this round of proofing, preheat the oven to 180°C. Bake the proofed rolls for 15–20 minutes.

8. In the meantime, prepare the glaze by beating cream cheese on medium speed using the paddle attachment of your stand mixer. Add sugar, milk and vanilla bean paste, then beat for about 3 minutes, until all the ingredients are well incorporated.

9. Spread the cream cheese glaze onto the rolls while they are still hot. Serve warm.

I love a good *kaya* bun, especially if it is soft and springy. The *tangzhong* method requires you to cook a bit of the flour with milk and make it into a roux before adding it to the rest of the dough. Some would call it the Asian starter in bread-making. You can attempt to make your own *kaya* but I prefer to choose my battles and work on the dough instead. Swap the *kaya* for red bean paste if that's what you prefer.

KAYA BUNS

Makes 9 buns

INGREDIENTS

TANGZHONG

20 g bread flour
100 ml milk

DOUGH

250 g bread flour
20 g rye flour
40 g castor sugar
5 g full cream milk powder
4 g instant dried yeast
1 egg
30 g whipping cream
5 tsp milk
100 g *tangzhong*
25 g unsalted butter, chilled and cut into small cubes
5 g salt

FILLING

300 g coconut egg jam (*kaya*), chilled

EGG WASH & TOPPING

1 egg
2 Tbsp milk
Sesame seeds for topping

METHOD

1. Prepare the *tangzhong* by cooking flour and milk together in a saucepan over medium heat, stirring with a spatula until a thick white paste forms. Remove from the heat and let it cool to room temperature for about 15 minutes before using.

2. For the dough, combine both flours, sugar, milk powder and yeast into a stand mixer's mixing bowl. Using the hook attachment, mix the dry ingredients together on low speed. Combine the egg, whipping cream, milk and *tangzhong* together in another bowl and whisk lightly.

3. Gradually add the wet ingredients to the dry ingredients, increasing the speed to medium as the dough comes together. Knead for about 8 minutes before adding butter and salt. Continue kneading for another 10–15 minutes.

4. Remove any dough from the hook attachment to combine with the rest of the dough and shape into a ball using your hands. Lightly grease the same mixing bowl with some vegetable oil, place the dough in it and cover with cling film. Let rest for an hour.

5. In the meantime, scoop a teaspoonful of coconut egg jam into your hands and roll into a ball. Make 9 balls and arrange spaced apart on a tray. Chill the balls in the refrigerator so that they are easy to handle later on.

6. Lightly dust your countertop or work surface with flour. Punch down the proofed dough to deflate it and divide into 9 equal pieces. You may weigh them if you prefer accuracy. Roll each piece into a ball, then use a rolling pin to flatten it evenly into a 7.5-cm disc. Place a chilled jam ball in its centre, then bring the sides together by crimping them. Place the dough ball seam side down and gently roll it around to smoothen the seam. Repeat to make 8 more dough balls.

7. Grease a 20-cm (8-in) square baking tin with butter and arrange the dough balls neatly in it. Let rest for another hour.

8. Preheat the oven to 160°C. Gently whisk egg and milk together, then brush the egg wash over the buns. Sprinkle with sesame seeds and bake for 15–20 minutes until golden brown.

9. Let cool for about an hour in the tin before transferring buns to a wire rack. Allow buns to cool completely before serving.

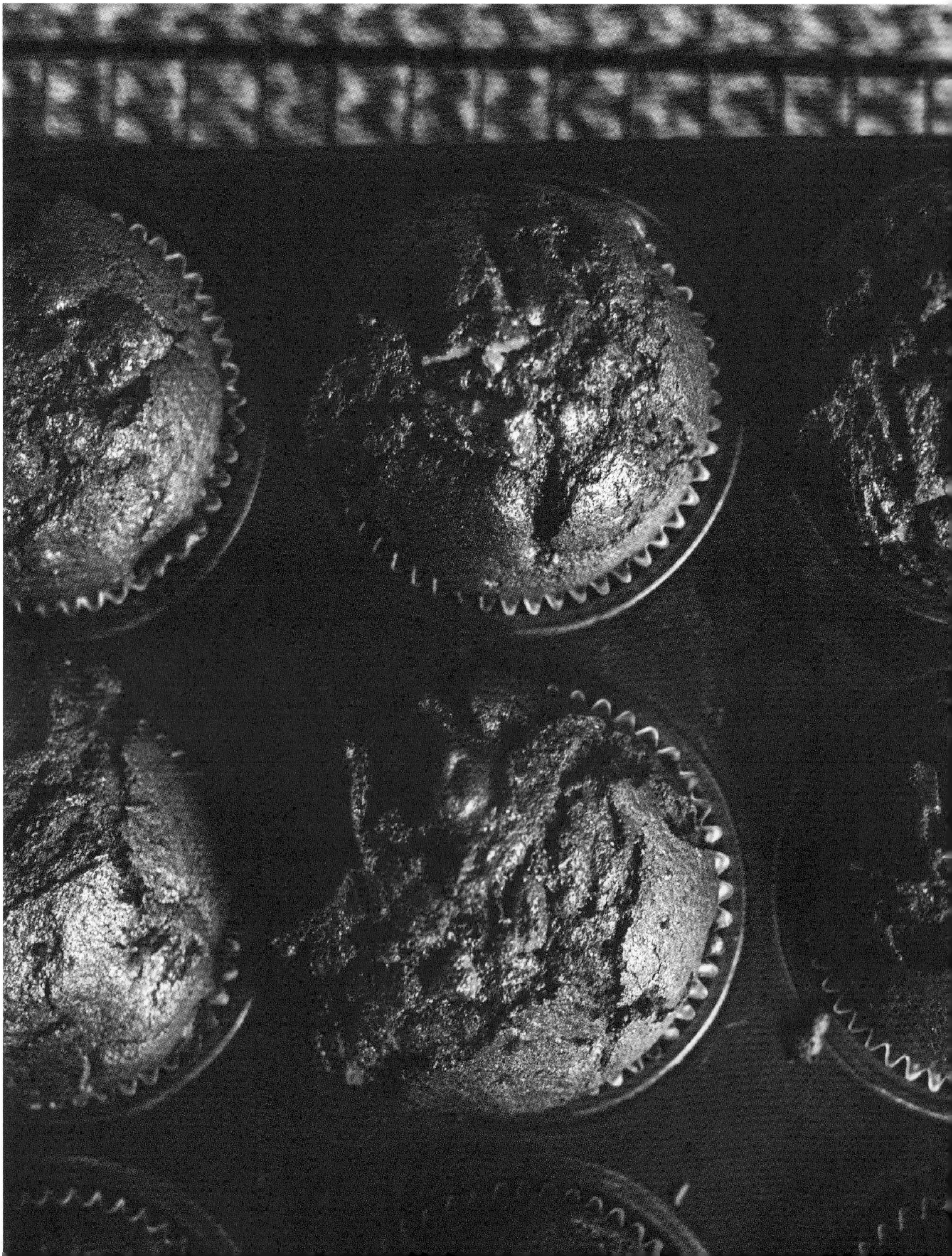

#sweetlikehoney

In 2019, a friend came to me with a proposition of selling cookies together during Hari Raya. Here's the thing: I had never tried selling my bakes no matter how much I baked or had been asked if I took orders. I decided to take the plunge and took her up on the offer. We baked at her place almost everyday for two weeks during the fasting month, churning out a total of about 10,000 cookies for packing into 150 bottles. I've heard someone say that these cookies are bought to be hidden in the room, not to be served to guests.

CHOCOLATE CHIP COOKIES

Makes about 60 cookies

INGREDIENTS

1 medium egg
5 g vanilla extract
10 g coffee emulco
250 g unsalted butter, at room temperature
100 g light brown sugar
100 g castor sugar
100 g all-purpose flour
50 g ground almond
5 g baking soda
10 g baking powder
5 g salt
50 g oats
200 g semi-sweet chocolate chips

METHOD

1. In a small bowl, beat egg together with coffee emulco and vanilla extract. Set aside.

2. Using an electric mixer with a paddle attachment, cream butter and both sugars together on medium speed until pale, light and fluffy. Gradually add the egg mixture and beat until well combined.

3. In a separate bowl, sift together flour, ground almond, baking soda, baking powder and salt. Add oats and lightly mix them in. To the butter-egg mixture, add the dry ingredients in 3 portions, stirring to combine well after each addition. Stop mixing once there are no traces of flour, then fold in chocolate chips.

4. Wrap cookie dough in cling film and shape it like a log. Rest the dough in the refrigerator or freezer for at least one hour until ready to bake. This step is crucial for achieving a crispy cookie.

5. Preheat the oven to 160°C. Scoop a tablespoonful of cookie dough, roll it into a ball and place on a lined baking tray. Repeat to use up the dough, arranging the balls spaced apart in neat rows.

6. Bake for 20 minutes or until crispy and golden brown.

When I first began baking, I was intrigued by this beautiful and rich red velvety cake, which was trendy in Singapore in the early 2010s. It was red velvet this, red velvet that for everything, but I can be a purist sometimes, preferring to return to a classic version of this Southern American treat. This red velvet cupcake also stole the heart of my husband; he still requests it from time to time, knowing that it's a treat worth waiting for.

RED VELVET CUPCAKES

Makes 12 cupcakes

INGREDIENTS

3 Tbsp dried coconut flakes
125 g cake flour
10 g Dutch-processed cocoa powder
$1/4$ tsp baking powder
$1/4$ tsp salt
120 ml buttermilk
1 Tbsp liquid red food coloring
60 g unsalted butter, at room temperature
120 g castor sugar
1 large egg, beaten
$1/2$ tsp vanilla extract
$1/2$ tsp baking soda
$1/2$ tsp apple cider vinegar

CREAM CHEESE FROSTING

227 g cream cheese, at room temperature
1 Tbsp castor sugar
1 tsp vanilla extract
117 g whipping cream

METHOD

1. Preheat the oven to 180°C. Line a muffin tray with paper liners.

2. Toast the coconut flakes in a dry frying pan, letting the sugar in the flakes caramelise and charring the edges lightly. When they are slightly browned, set aside to cool.

3. Sift flour, cocoa powder, baking powder and salt together in a medium bowl and set aside. In a measuring jug, combine buttermilk and food colouring, then set aside.

4. Using an electric mixer with a paddle attachment, cream butter and sugar on medium speed until pale yellow. Slowly add the beaten egg so that the fat from the yolk and butter will emulsify with the egg white. Add vanilla extract and beat on low speed to incorporate.

5. To the creamed mixture, add buttermilk in 2 equal portions, alternating with the dry ingredients and beating to combine. Quickly add baking soda and apple cider vinegar and mix until well incorporated.

6. Spoon batter equally into the prepared muffin cups and bake for 15–20 minutes, or until a skewer inserted into the centre of a cupcake comes out clean. Transfer to a wire rack and let cupcakes cool completely before frosting them.

7. In the meantime, cut cream cheese into cubes. Using an electric mixer with a paddle attachment, beat cream cheese until it resembles beaten butter, beginning on low speed at first and gradually increasing the speed. With the mixer on low speed, add sugar and vanilla extract, then slowly pour in whipping cream and beat until the frosting reaches stiff peaks.

8. Spoon the frosting into a piping bag either fitted with a tip of your choice or simply cut at the tip. Pipe onto cooled cupcakes and sprinkle generously with toasted coconut flakes. Serve with a nice cup of tea or coffee.

Café hopping was huge back in 2013. Small independent cafés began popping up in Singapore like mushrooms, serving coffee and cakes that were even more delicious than those by big coffee chains. I was a fresh graduate and had just started my first job, so I found solace in spending my weekends at cafés having a nice hot mug of long black along with a fudgy chocolate muffin. When I left my job to pursue photography as a career, I realised my café-hopping lifestyle had to stop. This muffin recipe, though, brings me back to my younger days of sipping pricey coffee as though money grew on trees.

FUDGY JUMBO CHOCOLATE MUFFINS

Makes 12 muffins

INGREDIENTS

125 g coconut oil
250 g castor sugar
3 large eggs
1 Tbsp vanilla extract
250 ml plain yoghurt
250 g all-purpose flour
115 g Dutch-processed cocoa powder
1 Tbsp baking powder
1/2 tsp baking soda
1/2 tsp sea salt
1 1/2 cups chocolate chunks or chocolate chips

METHOD

1. Preheat the oven to 160°C. Line a muffin tray with paper liners.

2. Using an electric mixer, cream coconut oil and sugar together on medium speed until the mixture is pale yellow and sugar granules are dissolved. Beat in eggs one at a time, then add vanilla extract and yoghurt, mixing until well incorporated.

3. In a bowl, combine flour, cocoa powder, baking powder, baking soda and salt. Add the dry ingredients to the wet mixture in 3 equal portions, folding each portion into the batter until well combined. Though you don't have to worry about muffins being dense or heavy, because they are essentially an easier way of making cupcakes, stop mixing once the dry ingredients are incorporated.

4. Fold in chocolate chunks or chips to evenly distribute them in the batter. Spoon batter equally into the prepared muffin cups and bake for 20 minutes, or until a skewer inserted into the centre of a muffin comes out clean.

5. Remove from the heat and transfer to a wire rack to cool. Serve warm.

Shortly after the end of my *MasterChef Singapore* journey, I was invited by CNA to cook for the premiere of their *Becoming Singapore* documentary. *Ondeh-ondeh* flavoured cake is not anything new or fancy — there are plenty of bakeries and home bakers out there who sell it. For the event, however, I tweaked my red velvet cake recipe to feature the richness of fresh coconut milk along with fresh pandan juice. The result is an amazingly soft, moist and elevated version of this cake.

ONDEH-ONDEH CAKE BARS

Makes about 12 bars

INGREDIENTS

10 pandan leaves
120 ml fresh coconut milk
114 g unsalted butter, at room temperature
150 g castor sugar
2 large eggs
100 g cake flour
80 g all-purpose flour
5 g salt
5 g baking powder
Coconut flakes, toasted, for garnishing

SYRUP

100 g palm sugar (*gula melaka*)
60 ml water

FROSTING

125 g cream cheese, at room temperature
120 ml whipping cream
15 g castor sugar
5 g vanilla extract

METHOD

1. Preheat the oven to 180°C. Grease and line a 20-cm (8-in) square baking tin with baking paper.

2. In a food processor, blend pandan leaves and coconut milk together to get a vivid green mixture. Strain the mixture through a muslin cloth, squeezing the pulp hard to ensure all the pandan flavour is extracted. Set aside.

3. Using an electric mixer with a paddle attachment, cream butter and sugar until pale and fluffy. Lightly beat eggs in a separate measuring jug before gradually adding to the creamed butter. Beat until eggs emulsify with the creamed butter.

4. In a separate bowl, sift both flours, salt and baking powder together. To the creamed mixture, add the dry ingredients in 3 equal portions, alternating with the pandan coconut milk and beating to combine. Stop mixing once all the dry ingredients are fully incorporated.

5. Pour the batter evenly into the prepared tray, using an offset spatula to smoothen the surface. Tap the tray a few times against the countertop to knock out any air bubbles, then bake for 20–25 minutes, or until a skewer inserted into the centre of the cake comes out clean.

6. Place a wire rack on top of the baking tin and flip the cake onto the wire rack. Without removing the tin, leave the cake to cool completely before unmoulding and slicing into bars.

7. Prepare the syrup. In a saucepan, heat palm sugar and water and simmer until the sugar is dissolved. Let cool and set aside.

8. For the frosting, use an electric mixer with a paddle attachment to beat cream cheese until fluffy. In a separate bowl, whisk whipping cream, sugar and vanilla extract until soft peaks form. Add the whipped cream to the cream cheese and fold it in carefully.

9. Transfer frosting to a piping bag and pipe onto the cake bars as desired. Drizzle with palm sugar syrup and garnish with toasted coconut flakes before serving.

When I was younger, my sisters would often get me to help out whenever they needed an extra hand in the kitchen. I was like a trainee cook following the orders of the head chef. My second sister, Malisa, is the pastry chef of the family. She would make cakes and bakes that seem daunting to do appear easy. When big coffee chains in Singapore began selling New York cheesecakes at eight dollars a slice — somewhat of a luxury — Malisa decided to make her own. I would usually be tasked with crushing the digestive biscuits. Eventually I memorised the recipe after watching her prepare it so many times.

NEW YORK CHEESECAKE

Makes a 20-cm round cake

INGREDIENTS

200 g chocolate digestive biscuits

80 g melted butter

678 g cream cheese, at room temperature

200 g castor sugar

1 tsp vanilla extract

Juice of $1/2$ lemon

3 large eggs

200 g sour cream

METHOD

1. Preheat the oven to 180°C. Line the bottom of a 20-cm (8-in) springform cake tin with baking paper.

2. To make the cheesecake base, use a food processor to blitz digestive biscuits into fine crumbs. Add butter and mix well. Spread and press the biscuit mixture onto the base of the prepared cake tin to form a crust about 1 cm thick. Bake for 10 minute, then set aside to cool. Keep the oven preheated at 180°C.

3. Using an electric mixer with a paddle attachment, beat cream cheese and sugar for 3-4 minutes until fluffy. Add vanilla extract and lemon juice, then beat to combine. Beat in eggs one at a time, making sure to scrape the bottom of the bowl as you mix. Add sour cream and mix until combined.

4. Wrap aluminium foil around the outside of the cake tin to prevent any leakage. Pour the cheesecake filling into the cake tin and use an offset spatula to smoothen the surface. Sit the tin in a deep baking tray.

5. Fill the tray with hot water to cover half of the baking tin's height before covering the tray with aluminium foil. Bake for an hour, then remove the top foil and bake uncovered for another 30-40 minutes, until the top is lightly golden brown and a skewer inserted into the centre of the cake comes out clean.

6. At this point, DO NOT TAKE THE CAKE OUT OF THE OVEN. Switch off the heat and leave the oven door slightly ajar by propping it open with a wooden spoon. Let the cake rest in the oven for 45 minutes – this will prevent it from cracking due to any sudden change in temperature.

7. Remove from the water bath and let the cake cool for another 2 hours before chilling in the refrigerator overnight. This cake is best served chilled with coffee.

8. This recipe is extremely versatile. You could use Oreo biscuits in place of digestive biscuits for the base and add in chunks of mini Oreo biscuits to make an Oreo cheesecake! It also works with any other flavoured biscuits.

I must admit, I have a bad case of sweet tooth. I love reaching for bread and Nutella as an easy dessert after a dinner. Other times, I bake a cake at the start of the week to have dessert taken care of for the rest of the week. On the weekends, I experiment with new recipes so that my mum and I have something to munch on at teatime. Perhaps I would have been a pastry chef and owned a bakery in another life. This sea salt chocolate tart is one of the simplest desserts anyone can make.

SEA SALT CHOCOLATE TART

Makes one 20-cm tart

INGREDIENTS

TART SHELL

225 g all-purpose flour
100 g unsalted butter, cut into cubes and chilled
A pinch of salt
3 Tbsp cold water

CHOCOLATE FILLING

300 g double cream
2 tsp castor sugar
A pinch of fine sea salt
20 g unsalted butter
200 g dark chocolate (at least 70% cocoa)

METHOD

1. Preheat the oven to 180°C.

2. Sift flour into a large bowl. Use your fingertips to rub butter into the flour to create a mixture resembling fine breadcrumbs. When you're making shortcrust pastry, it's really important to use cold butter – it helps the flour proteins absorb less water, preventing the formation of gluten.

3. Stir in salt, then add 2-3 tablespoonfuls of water and mix to form a firm dough. Tip the dough onto a lightly floured surface and knead it gently and briefly. Do not overwork the dough because you do not want gluten to form. Ensure the dough has a smooth surface, then roll it into a ball. Wrap in cling film and refrigerate for up to one day, or freeze it for up to a week before using.

4. Lightly dust your countertop or work surface with flour and roll out the pastry into a circle about 0.5 cm thick. Gently transfer to a 20-cm (8-in) tart tin, making sure the sides of the tin are fully covered and using a knife to trim any excess pastry. Line the tart shell with baking paper, fill it with dried beans, then blind bake for 10-15 minutes. Remove the beans and paper before baking for another 15 minutes until golden brown. Set aside to cool while you make the filling.

5. Place cream, sugar and salt in a saucepan and bring to the boil. As soon as the mixture boils, turn off the heat and stir in butter and chocolate until well combined. Pour into the tart shell and leave to cool at room temperature for 2 hours before refrigerating it.

6. Chill overnight and sprinkle with more sea salt before serving.

acknowledgements

My biggest thanks would first and foremost be for my husband, Faeez, who has always been my number one supporter since I embarked on this food journey. My time in *MasterChef Singapore* coincided with the time we courted and dated. The month-long filming took place six months before our wedding, and then a month into marriage, my debut on *MasterChef Singapore* premiered on television. For all the times I failed in the kitchen, he was always there to remind me that he was not a judge. And for all the times I successfully served up meals, he was there to give me words of encouragement and gratitude.

I would also like to thank my mother, Ibu, whose many recipes I adapted and made better (though she denies this). Thank you for imparting some knowledge of food to me and trying to be patient when I asked you to slow down your cooking just so I could note down the amount correctly, instead of just "*agak-agak*".

My eldest sister, Shamsynar, thank you for elevating my palate, and teaching me how to eat expensive and appreciate good food. Without you I would not have access to the knowledge of food I have now. For all the times you fed me while raising three hungry kids and caring for a husband, thank you.

I would also like to thank Munn Iskandar (@munnisk), my trusted photography assistant, for helping with the photos of myself, which I could not possibly shoot on my own.

Last but not least, thank you to my best friend, Izzati, for always being there for me no matter what.

weightsandmeasures

Quantities for this book are given in Metric and American (spoon and cup) measures. Standard spoon and cup measurements used are: 1 teaspoon = 5 ml, 1 tablespoon = 15 ml, 1 cup = 250 ml. All measures are level unless otherwise stated.

LIQUID AND VOLUME MEASURES

Metric	Imperial	American
5 ml	$1/6$ fl oz	1 teaspoon
10 ml	$1/3$ fl oz	1 dessertspoon
15 ml	$1/2$ fl oz	1 tablespoon
60 ml	2 fl oz	$1/4$ cup (4 tablespoons)
85 ml	$2^1/2$ fl oz	$1/3$ cup
90 ml	3 fl oz	$3/8$ cup (6 tablespoons)
125 ml	4 fl oz	$1/2$ cup
180 ml	6 fl oz	$3/4$ cup
250 ml	8 fl oz	1 cup
300 ml	10 fl oz ($1/2$ pint)	$1^1/4$ cups
375 ml	12 fl oz	$1^1/2$ cups
435 ml	14 fl oz	$1^3/4$ cups
500 ml	16 fl oz	2 cups
625 ml	20 fl oz (1 pint)	$2^1/2$ cups
750 ml	24 fl oz ($1^1/5$ pints)	3 cups
1 litre	32 fl oz ($1^3/5$ pints)	4 cups
1.25 litres	40 fl oz (2 pints)	5 cups
1.5 litres	48 fl oz ($2^2/5$ pints)	6 cups
2.5 litres	80 fl oz (4 pints)	10 cups

DRY MEASURES

Metric	Imperial
30 grams	1 ounce
45 grams	$1^1/2$ ounces
55 grams	2 ounces
70 grams	$2^1/2$ ounces
85 grams	3 ounces
100 grams	$3^1/2$ ounces
110 grams	4 ounces
125 grams	$4^1/2$ ounces
140 grams	5 ounces
280 grams	10 ounces
450 grams	16 ounces (1 pound)
500 grams	1 pound, $1^1/2$ ounces
700 grams	$1^1/2$ pounds
800 grams	$1^3/4$ pounds
1 kilogram	2 pounds, 3 ounces
1.5 kilograms	3 pounds, $4^1/2$ ounces
2 kilograms	4 pounds, 6 ounces

OVEN TEMPERATURE

	°C	°F	Gas Regulo
Very slow	120	250	1
Slow	150	300	2
Moderately slow	160	325	3
Moderate	180	350	4
Moderately hot	190/200	370/400	5/6
Hot	210/220	410/440	6/7
Very hot	230	450	8
Super hot	250/290	475/550	9/10

LENGTH

Metric	Imperial
0.5 cm	$1/4$ inch
1 cm	$1/2$ inch
1.5 cm	$3/4$ inch
2.5 cm	1 inch